MW00608592

Mechanical Trading Systems

Mechanical Trading Systems

Pairing Trader Psychology with Technical Analysis

RICHARD L. WEISSMAN

WILEY

John Wiley & Sons, Inc.

For my wife, Pamela Nations-Weissman, whose vision inspired this manuscript, and also for my parents, whose belief and support guided me through the early years

Every battle is won before it is ever fought.

—Sun Tzu

Contents

Preface

In 1987 my father and I purchased a seat on the New York Futures Exchange for $100 and established a trading account with $25,000. The goal, he explained, was to make $2,500 a week. Although this seemed like an extraordinary annualized return on investment, I had heard of legendary traders who had taken meager sums and transformed them into vast fortunes, and so I embarked on a journey that eventually culminated in the publication of this book.

I wish I could tell you that this book contains the secrets of how I accomplished that formidable goal, but I never did learn how to consistently produce even a 100 percent average annualized rate of return on my capital. I will say that if I had somehow accomplished that goal I would probably have very little knowledge to offer the typical trader. Instead my journey was a difficult one in which I gradually learned that trying to earn several hundred percent on my capital annually was, for me at least, a recipe for disaster.

And yet if I had known what I now understand about realistic rates of return on investment vis-à-vis risks taken to achieve those returns, I might not have chosen speculation as a career, and that path has given me far more than mere financial rewards. It has taught me to be open-minded, patient, objective, consistent, disciplined, even-minded, and nonattached to the results of my actions. In addition, it taught me how to survive as a trader while suffering from being severely undercapitalized.

I am certain that there must be numerous practical methods accessible to traders that allow them to produce respectable overall rates of return on their capital while minimizing the risk of ruin. However, to this day, the only method that I have been able to impart successfully to professional traders is that of employing mechanical trading systems based on mathematical technical analysis. Such mechanical trading systems allow the development of comprehensive, detailed trading plans that include rules of entry, exit, and price risk management. More important, they enable the backtesting and forward testing of a particular strategy's results prior to the commitment of capital. This, in turn, aids in fostering the discipline necessary to weather the inevitable losses inherent in employment of any trading program.

This book will not show readers how to turn $10,000 into $1 million in one year's time. I believe that system developers advocating their ability to generate such rates of return are charlatans, victims of curve-fitted trading systems, or theoreticians blind to the risk of ruin entailed in the achievement of such spectacular returns. Instead of spectacular risks and returns, I offer simple trading systems that, because of that very simplicity, are quite robust in terms of generating overall positive rates of return while simultaneously minimizing the risk of ruin. Although the proprietary strategies I personally trade differ from those employed in this book, the systems offered herein are simple enough to have a significant probability of ensuring the achievement of similar, moderately successful results in the future. That being said, the methodologies examined herein are certainly not intended as "holy grails" of trading, but instead are offered as prototypes to motivate and guide readers in developing systems that match their individual temperaments.

Critics of books on trading system development suggest that no one would give away a successful trading system and that if a profitable system were given away, it would no longer work since everyone would be using it. Such criticism suggests a naivete regarding market dynamics and trader psychology. This book argues that the primary reason for failure as a speculator is a lack of disciplined adherence to successful trading and price risk management strategies as opposed to an inability to discover profitable trading methodologies. The text shows that the development of rock-solid discipline is among the most challenging endeavors to which a trader can aspire. If this were not the case, anyone could master discipline and there would be no financial rewards associated with successful speculation.

When mechanical trading systems were first introduced into the arsenal of trading tools, traders interested in utilizing such tools would have needed programming expertise, a strong background in mathematical technical analysis, and iron-willed discipline. Over time, the trading system software developed by market data vendors has become simpler and more user friendly, so that now nonprogrammers with only a rudimentary understanding of mathematical technical analysis can successfully create and backtest simple trading systems such as those offered throughout this manuscript. It is for this reason that I have chosen to showcase CQG's backtesting and optimization software as opposed to more "programmer-oriented" system development solutions.

Although the primary intention of this book is to provide tools to aid relative newcomers in quickly identifying their trading biases and shortcomings, the feedback I have received while presenting this material to professional traders suggests that a detailed examination of the personality traits common to the three basic trader types—(long to intermediate term) trend-following, (intermediate-term) mean reversion, and short-term trading (swing and day traders)—along with a strict adherence to specific kinds of trading systems can foster a psychological flexibility that enables traders to succeed in all kinds of trading environments: countertrending, choppy, or trending. In addition, my hope is that the text proves valuable to institutional investors, affluent private investors, and others participating in investment vehicles that contain a systematic trading component.

Through this framework of "reprogramming the trader," the book examines the development process for mechanical trading systems. This process includes reasons for their popularity, the dangers in system development and how to avoid them, how backtesting and forward testing of trading systems aids in quantification of price risk, and methods of improving rates of return on investment without significantly increasing risk.

Throughout, I have striven to progress in a linear fashion from basic, rudimentary concepts to those of greater complexity. Nevertheless, in certain instances, to ensure both the reader's comprehension of a particular concept's utility as well as to preserve the coherence and integrity of the material, I was forced to introduce ideas that traditionally would have been included in later chapters. Wherever this was unavoidable, I have reiterated the concepts in the later chapters or referred the reader back to the earlier chapter.

Chapter 1 defines mathematical technical analysis, distinguishes it from classical technical analysis, and shows the psychological reasons behind why it works. Then it explains why mathematical technical analysis is an ideal building block in the development of mechanical trading systems as opposed to either fundamental analysis or interpretive technical analysis. Finally, the chapter dispels the myth of mechanical trading systems as an easy method of generating profits.

Chapter 2 looks at the two basic flavors of mathematical technical indicators: those attempting to capitalize on the market's propensity toward mean reversion (i.e., oscillators), and indicators that profit from trending price activity (e.g., moving averages). The chapter then shows how technical indicators can be transformed into comprehensive trading systems through the inclusion of various risk quantification parameters such as volatility bands and percentage value of the trading instrument.

Chapter 3 examines trend-following trading systems and shows how even the most simplistic of systems can produce a respectable rate of return while enduring relatively moderate worst peak-to-valley drawdowns in equity. It also discusses why certain asset classes tend to trend more than others and concludes with a detailed exposition of the personality traits necessary to succeed as a trend-following trader.

Chapter 4 looks at simple intermediate-term mean reversion trading systems. It examines why certain asset classes display a greater propensity toward mean reversion than others and includes examples of nondirectionally biased mean reversion systems and mean reversion systems that employ a trend-following filter. The chapter concludes with an exposition of the personality traits required for success as an intermediate-term mean reversion trader.

Chapter 5 explores short-term—including swing and day trading—systems and the personality traits needed to succeed with these strategies. As with Chapters 3 and 4, the chapter examines backtested case studies and analyzes the personality traits best suited for success with these strategies.

Chapter 6 acts as a comprehensive review of the major categories of trader types (trend-following, mean reversion) as well as the typical time frames (long term, intermediate term, swing, and day trading) in which they operate. The chapter examines the various flaws in trader psychology—fearfulness, impatience, greed, lack of discipline, and so on, within the context of these personality types and trading time frames—then shows how to identify these weaknesses by examining the trader's personality traits and trading style. Once readers have successfully identified their innate trading personality, a step-by-step transformational process via utilization of different types of mechanical trading systems and psychological tools is outlined.

Chapter 7 examines the many benefits offered by mechanical trading systems that have not been previously addressed. Then the text looks at the downside to system development and how to resolve these problems: data curve fitting, parameter curve fitting, data integrity issues, and underestimation of commissions and slippage. The chapter also examines the benefits and limitations of optimization studies, development of trading system philosophy statements, and the pros and cons of various methodologies for measuring trading system performance.

Chapter 8 discusses the pros and cons of various traditional price risk management methods, such as stop loss and volumetric price risk management. Coverage of volumetric price risk includes both Martingale and anti-Martingale position sizing techniques, such as fixed fractional position sizing and value at risk. Other price risk management techniques covered include the study of worst-backtested peak-to-valley equity drawdowns, "static" volumetric limits, stress testing and system stop losses as a percentage of total equity under management. Finally, the chapter examines the psychological aspects of price risk management and shows how utilization of mechanical trading systems can aid in fostering confidence during drawdowns.

Chapter 9 looks at improving the overall rate of return through three methods:

1. The addition of various low and/or negatively correlated assets, such as crude oil and foreign exchange futures, into a single trading system
2. The staggering of parameter set trigger levels for the same system
3. The combination of mean reversion and trend-following systems within a single trading account or fund

The chapter then concludes with an examination of the psychological benefits gained through expansion beyond one's "trading comfort zone."

Chapter 10 examines how a trader's knowledge and experience can be utilized within the framework of a mechanical trading system. The pros and cons of increasing or decreasing position size among assets within a large trading book—e.g., buying one E-mini S&P contract instead of 10—based on various objectively quantifiable "discretionary" factors such as increases in historical volatility, exceeding of worst peak-to-valley drawdowns in equity, and so on, as well as "fuzzier" discretionary elements, including contrary opinion, fundamental market analysis, and headline news events, are covered in detail.

Chapter 11 examines the link between mechanical trading systems and transformational psychology, covering in detail issues such as self-worth, single-mindedness, discipline, nonattachment to the results of one's actions, and recognition and releasing of old emotional patterns. The chapter concludes by examining skills mastered in the realm of trading and applying them to life in general to achieve greater harmony.

It is this final point—the achievement of a more harmonious outlook on life in general—that is my most sincere and fervent hope for readers. Without it, trading is the worthy pursuit of a livelihood. With it, the truly motivated trader's desire to master discipline is elevated to the quest of self-discovery.

Acknowledgments

I believe that all of an individual's accomplishments are integrally linked to the totality of his or her life experiences. As such, all acknowledgments necessarily fall short of their goal. Having said this, I would like to thank family, friends, and colleagues for their support and encouragement in the writing of this book.

In addition, I would like to thank Richard Hom, who has acted as a brilliant sounding board for various concepts through the years; Robert Weber, for his editorial insights; Dr. Kurtay Ogunc, Marcia Epley, Jesse Van Luvan, Barbara Rockefeller, Dr. Russell Grimwood, Neil Brown, Marsha Lipton, Frederic Bettan, Luis Castellanos, and Douglas Coyne; my students; The Oxford Princeton Programme; Alex Moffett; Stan Yabroff of CQG; and my editors at John Wiley, Kevin Commins, Lara Murphy, and Matt Kellen.

I also wish to acknowledge my indebtedness to all the authors listed in this book's reference list. If this book has added anything to the fields of mechanical trading systems, trader psychology, and technical analysis, it is as a direct result of their work. Finally, I would like to acknowledge the depth of my gratitude to Sogyal Rinpoche, H.H. Chetsang Rinpoche, and Drikung Kagyu Sangha, whose works have inspired and transformed my work and my life.

Mechanical Trading Systems

CHAPTER 1

Dispelling Myths and Defining Terms

Mathematical Technical Analysis and Mechanical Trading Systems

Appearances often are deceiving.

—Aesop

DISPELLING THE MYTHS: THE INEFFICIENT MARKET AND THE HARD ROAD TO PROFITS

The Inefficient Market

If traders behaved in a rational manner, the market would be efficient and trading would offer few opportunities for consistent profit, but time and again market participants behave illogically, basing their decisions on emotional responses. Perhaps the most compelling evidence in terms of market participant irrationality is put forth by proponents of behavioral finance. Behavioral finance, when traders or investors base decisions on emotions, is diametrically opposed to theories of random market behavior and efficient market hypothesis, which assumes that all market participants behave rationally.[1]

Recent acceptance of behavioral finance by the academic community[2] validates what technicians have known for well over 100 years: Market participants behave irrationally, and it is this emotionalism that leads to stable Paretian price distributions.[3] Such distributions are characterized by a greater propensity toward mean reversion than suggested by a random distribution, which technicians capitalize on with mean reversion tools, such as Wilder's Relative Strength Index, and amplified tails—also known as trends—which technicians profit from through trend-following tools, such as moving averages.[4]

Although the irrationality of markets is why technical analysis works, it

1

is also the greatest danger in the execution of a mechanical trading system. Traders must have the discipline to continuously behave in an unnatural, uncomfortable manner to consistently generate profits. This is why mechanical trading is difficult. Discipline and money management means acting like a machine. It means tempering emotionalism—few thrills or excitement, few of the life-affirming things that we as human beings seek. It sounds boring because, if done correctly, it *should* be boring. In part it is this lack of excitement that makes its successful execution so difficult. However, there are challenging aspects to all trading, even mechanical trading. The most obvious creative aspect of mechanical trading is the process of system development and refinement itself. In addition, in later chapters we will examine discretion over position sizing and how this lends itself to creativity.

Thus, the greatest obstacle to successful trading as a technician is not the ability to discover a successful trading strategy; rather, it stems from the inability of people to take trading signals generated by the mechanical system. Even if traders can train themselves to do the unnatural, uncomfortable thing by adhering to proscribed entry signals, the battle for self-mastery has only just begun; the ability to exit trades—whether those exits are with profits or with losses—as dictated by a mechanical trading system is clearly the most formidable obstacle faced by traders.

Taking the Trades: The Psychology of Entry

Successful trading in some ways requires an unlearning of many old psychological behavioral patterns. The vast majority of our life experiences prior to our decision to trade involve the avoidance of pain, error, mistakes, imperfections, and uncertainty and the seeking of pleasure, excitement, approval, and perfection. These previously learned psychological patterns lead us to seek out the "perfect" entry point, which often means either abandonment of our entry level when we discover its imperfections or an inability to execute entry orders due to our desire to wait for the elusive "perfect" entry price.[5]

In fact, successful entry levels often are diametrically opposed to the notion of a "perfect" price. Since the "perfect" entry would entail buying the low tick or selling short at the ultimate market high, this automatically rules out participation in any well-defined trend, because these trends almost always entail entry at recent highs or lows. And as stated earlier, trend-following systems are quite profitable because they enable participation in the amplified tails within a market's price distribution.

Exiting the Trades: With Profits and Losses

The vast majority of novice technicians focus almost entirely on tools to assist them in entering trades for the reasons stated above. What makes successful trading so elusive is the lack of focus on exiting positions either with profits or with losses. Behavioral finance proposes that one reason for lack of success in exit strategies is an irrational emphasis on entry price.[6] This focus on entry price leads to exiting profitable trades prematurely. We tend to think of our entry price as a comfortable, "realistic" level—after all, didn't we recently enter at that price? This emphasis on entry price gives us a sense of comfort since we are able to focus on a quantifiable, known reference point. As profits accumulate and we move farther from our comfortable reference point, our fear of reversal becomes more acute and our confidence necessarily deteriorates. And so our irrational fear of allowing small profits to turn into losses prevents the realization of large profits.

This same emphasis on entry levels gives us a false sense of security as trades begin to deteriorate. We remind ourselves that our entry level was only recently achieved and therefore assume that a return to this level is highly probable. This irrational emphasis on our psychological reference point produces an unfounded sense of confidence and allows losses to escalate from manageable to catastrophic levels.

This psychological framework of "natural" and "comfortable" trading—using entry levels as a reference point—ensures small profits and large losses. Success in trading means training ourselves to fight our "natural" psychological frameworks by being "comfortable" with the unknown future as opposed to the traditional comfortable reference point of our entry price. In reprogramming ourselves to be comfortable with the unknowable and uncertain future, it helps to remind ourselves that the entry level is significant to us alone and that the sense of discomfort that we feel as the market moves into previously unknown territory is entirely subjective and illusory.

In summary, this use of our entry price as a reference point makes us fearful when we should be most confident—when the market is telling us that we are right by increasing our unrealized profits—and gives us an erroneous sense of security when we should be most cautious. And so we cut our profits and let losses run, which of course is the exact opposite of successful trend trading. This book offers a multitude of psychological and mechanical techniques intended to replace destructive behavioral patterns with ones that foster success in trading as well as a more harmonious outlook on life in general.

TECHNICAL ANALYSIS: A DEFINITION[7]

The goal of technical analysis often is said to be the forecasting of future price "trends." I would qualify this definition so that the term *trend* encompasses all types of market activity, including trending, countertrending, and sideways price action. The basic precept in all technical analysis is that by studying past price history and evaluating volume or number of trades and open interest or the number of contracts outstanding, traders can forecast future price "trends" and identify low-risk/high-reward trading opportunities.

This broad definition can be further narrowed into two distinct subcategories: interpretative or subjective technical analysis and mathematical or objective technical analysis. Subjective or "classical" technical analysis attempts to capitalize on visual price history patterns that are subject to interpretation. Examples of this type of analysis include the head and shoulders pattern, inverted head and shoulders, along with various diagonal trend-line formations, including triangles, flags, and pennants.[8]

Although interpretive technical indicators cannot be quantified objectively, they are nonetheless powerful tools, enabling both the quantification of risk and the identification of valid market trends. Despite their usefulness, the identification of such visual patterns is entirely subjective, as the name "interpretative" suggests. As a result, the validity of such interpretative indicators cannot be statistically verified, and their utilization for mechanical trading systems is severely limited.

In stark contrast to interpretative technical indicators, the success or failure of mathematical technical indicators is always indisputable because the buy and sell signals that they generate are based on objective and immutable rules. The simplest and most popular of these types of indicators is the simple moving average.

The simple moving average is the average price of a specific data set. For example, if we were interested in knowing the 200-day simple moving average for U.S. dollar–Japanese yen (see Figure 1.1), we would add up the settlement prices of the prior 200 trading days and then divide the total by 200. Upon the completion of each new trading day, the data from the oldest day—201 trading days ago—drops from our moving average calculation and is replaced by the new settlement price, hence the term *moving average*.

The theory behind using a moving average is that if the market is in a significant uptrend, prices should not be weak enough to fall below the 200-day moving average. Once the market is weak enough to breach the moving average, this theoretically suggests the end of the old uptrend and start of a new downtrend.

Because this utilization of the moving average line not only produces objective trading signals but also quantifies risk, it is considered to be not only a technical indicator but also a mechanical trading system, albeit the most simplistic one imaginable. Since buy and sell signals are generated whenever the moving average line is violated, it is known as a stop-and-reverse trading system. It is a stop-and-reverse system because whenever the

FIGURE 1.1 Spot U.S. dollar–Japanese yen with 200-day moving average.
©2004 CQG, Inc. All rights reserved worldwide.

market becomes weak enough to close below the moving average line, we not only exit all existing long positions but also initiate new short positions.

Although a 200-day simple moving average is by no means the most successful mechanical trading system, it clearly illustrates what technicians mean when they speak of objective, mathematical indicators. It is this objectivity of trading signals derived from mathematical technical analysis that makes mathematical technical analysis the indispensable foundation of the vast majority of mechanical trading systems.

MECHANICAL TRADING SYSTEMS: A DEFINITION

Mechanical trading systems can be defined as methods of generating trading signals and quantifying risk that are independent of an individual trader's discretion. Although the advantages in utilizing a mechanical trading system are manifold, most market participants agree that their greatest benefit is the tempering of destructive trader "emotionalism"—which is considered to be the enemy of all successful market participants—from the decision-making process.

Obviously mechanical trading systems can be developed based on any number of objective criteria including interest rate differentials, gross domestic product, or earnings per share. Although this book in no way negates the validity of such fundamental tools in system development,[9] I do argue that an inherent limitation in using such tools is that they require an in-depth understanding of a particular market or trading instrument.

By contrast, mathematical technical indicators do not require any particular specialized knowledge of the underlying fundamentals affecting a particular market on the part of system developers. This absence of expertise thereby allows traders to apply their system as readily to Asian equities or live cattle, soybeans or foreign exchange, sugar or natural gas. Although obvious benefits gained by participating in diverse markets will be examined in detail later, for now let me suggest that diversification into various low to negatively correlated asset classes increases the likelihood of improved rates of return on investment and often reduces the severity of peak-to-valley drawdowns in equity.[10]

DEFINING THE TIME FRAMES

Often traders will define themselves by the time frame of their positions. The problem is that there is no universally accepted definition of what separates long, intermediate, and short-term traders. For the sake of simplicity and consistency, I will designate some time parameters to each of these terms. As used in this book, long-term traders are those who attempt to profit from trends lasting anywhere from 1 to 6 months. Intermediate-term traders are those who hold trades from 10 days to 1 month, and short-term traders are those holding positions for less than 10 days.

TECHNICAL ANALYSIS: WHY IT WORKS

As shown in later chapters, technical analysis can be used to develop two different types of mechanical trading systems: price-driven systems or indicator-driven systems (along with a combination of the two). Both types of trigger events can be used to produce successful trading systems because they capitalize on recurring psychological conditions in the market.

Psychological Significance of Price Triggers: Horizontal Support and Resistance Levels

To understand why technical analysis works in terms of market psychology, let us examine the heating oil futures market, which began trading on Nymex during the late 1970s.

The late 1970s and early 1980s marked a strong uptrend in energy prices. During the summer of 1979, heating oil futures tested the $1.05 per gallon region and then quickly returned to around $0.72/gallon. This failure to rise above $1.05/gallon defined that area as resistance, or the level at which the upward price momentum was thwarted.

Over the next few years, the market would again test the $1.05/gallon resistance level and again that price level would act as a ceiling, preventing penetration to higher price levels. In fact, the $1.05 level would be retested in 1981, 1982, and 1984 without being breached (see Figure 1.2).

In terms of market psychology, the $1.05/gallon level emerged as an important resistance mark and price trigger. Consider the significance of the $1.05 price level to various market participants. First we examine traders who bought $1.05 in anticipation of trend continuation. Instead of accepting a small loss as the rally gave way to retracement, some of these buyers actually suffered through the gut-wrenching despair of watching prices fall to $0.72/gallon. As the market again approached $1.05 their despair gave way to redemption, and they seized the chance to exit without a loss by offsetting their prior purchases with a break-even sale (see Chapter 3, Cutting the Tails of Our System's Distribution).

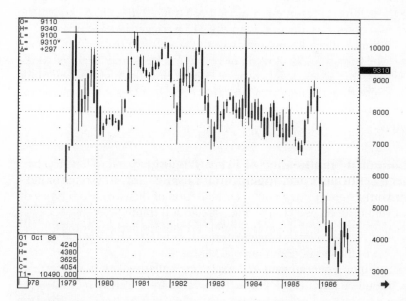

FIGURE 1.2 Rolling front-month Nymex heating oil futures showing $1.05/gal horizontal resistance.

Those who sold the $1.05 area obviously enjoyed superior market knowledge, and it is logical to assume that the majority of them realized a considerable profit by covering their short sale at lower levels for a profit. As the market again approached $1.05, they are even more aggressive in repeating what had proved a successful trade in the past since the market has now defined the $1.05 region as a low risk/high reward trading opportunity. (These traders can initiate short positions at $1.05; place a stop loss order at $1.06 and a limit order to close out the position with a profit just above $0.72.)

Consider those with sideline regret/remorse (see Chapter 3, Cutting the Tails of Our System's Distributing). These are players who anticipated the end of the bullish trend but failed to capitalize by selling at $1.05. As the market came off from the $1.05 level, they watched from the sidelines in anguish, fearing that selling after the market retreated from these levels represented too much risk and not enough reward. The resurgence to $1.05 signifies their redemption as well since they can now "sell the top" as they had originally hoped. There is a much greater likelihood of them executing sell orders this second time around, since the top is now a clearly defined price level as opposed to an amorphous sense of the market being "overvalued." (Note: All of these same psychological factors—break-even syndrome, sideline regret/remorse—apply to support levels in downtrends.)

Finally, what happens if the buying pressure becomes strong enough to satiate the selling represented by all of these trader types? In that case, the market psychology associated with the $1.05 trigger level is reversed as shorts with unrealized losses seek to exit positions at breakeven. Consequently when the market moves above the old resistance level at $1.05, then retests that price level, former sellers buy back short positions, thereby supporting the market against lower prices. This is why old resistance, once broken, becomes new support and old support becomes new resistance.

Psychological Significance of Price Triggers: Horizontal Support and Resistance Levels: Corrections

Another example of market psychology in relation to price triggers is the tendency of trends to experience temporary, countertrend reversals within the context of the larger dominant market trend.

Such minor countertrend reversals are called corrections, retracements, or pullbacks and typically are measured from the lowest low of the prior trend to the most recent highest high in bull market trends, or from the highest high of the prior trend to the most recent lowest low in bear market trends. The strength or weakness of the dominant market trend can be determined by the severity or mildness of these corrections.

The psychology behind market corrections is as follows. Hedgers and short-term countertrend traders establish countertrend positions into logical price target areas that are often long-term support or resistance levels, as discussed above. (Trend-following traders also may exit with profits at these logical price trigger levels.) As the market returns from its highs or lows, intermediate and short-term trend-followers take profits, accelerating the correction. Adding fuel to the corrective fire, the retreat from recent highs or lows is accompanied by a "shaking out" of weak or recent longs or shorts—those that are undercapitalized or have little tolerance for drawdowns in equity.

These corrective moves tend to climax at key retracement levels such as 38, 50, or 62 percent, because countertrend traders tend to take profits and trend-followers—that is, hedgers and long-term speculators—often add on to existing positions into these logical, low-risk/high-reward retracement levels.

The most infamous example of a correction against the dominant market trend was the crash of 1987. From the ultimate S&P 500 low of 1982 at 101.44 to the 1987 highs at 337.89, we can measure a bull move of 236.45 S&P 500 points. Dividing this price move by 50 percent we get 118.23 S&P 500 points. Adding 118.23 to the 1982 lows at 101.44 gives us 219.67. The ultimate low print of the so-called crash of 1987 was in fact 216.47—which lies just below a 50 percent correction of the prior bull move (see Figure 1.3). Consequently, I contend that this so-called crash was in fact nothing more than a pullback in the bull market. This example illustrates the severity and emotionalism that can accompany major corrections against the dominant trend.

Psychological Significance of Indicator-Driven Triggers

An indicator-driven trigger can be defined as an occurrence such as a price close above or below a moving average or the crossing of an oscillator above or below a significant level.[11] Because the significance of the trigger is directly proportionate to the emphasis that market participants place on the indicator, the more focus on the indicator, the greater the probability of impact on subsequent price activity. This is why deriders of technical analysis view it as a self-fulfilling prophecy. Although I agree that indicator-driven triggers often act as self-fulfilling prophecies, I do not believe that this in any way negates their utility. Instead, the indicators are like emotional barometers: The fact that there is such widespread

FIGURE 1.3   Monthly cash S&P 500 chart with retracements.

focus on indicator-driven triggers in some manner tunes various participants into emotions of fear, greed, and capitulation makes them an invaluable tool in price trend forecasting.

TYPES OF TECHNICAL INDICATORS: TREND-FOLLOWING AND MEAN REVERSION

Another common argument against technical analysis suggests price activity in commodity and financial markets is random.[12] In fact, instead of a random, bell-curved price distribution, most—around 70 percent—of the time,
prices trade in a sideways or range-bound pattern.[13] In statistical terms,
commodity and financial markets are said to be leptokurtic. That is, they
display a strong tendency toward mean reversion—in other words, prices
tend to cluster around the mean.

Why then are such a large portion of technical analysts and mechanical
trading systems dedicated to trend identification? The reason is because
when prices are not in this mean reversion mode, they tend to trend. In sta-

tistical terms, commodity and financial markets are leptokurtic with amplified tails—when they are not in their mean-reverting mode, they tend to display powerful and sustainable trends. These trends offer traders low-risk/high-reward opportunities, such that a single profitable trend-following trade often will offset numerous small losses, thereby resulting in an overall profitable trading system that experiences less than 50 percent winning trades.

The 200-day simple moving average examined earlier provides us with an excellent example of a trend-following indicator. Another popular variation on this mathematical trend-following indicator is known as the two-moving average crossover system (see Figure 1.4).

The two-moving-average crossover system entails the introduction of a second, shorter-term moving average, such as a 9-day simple moving average. Now instead of buying or selling whenever the market closes above or below the 200-day simple moving average, our trend-following trader establishes long positions whenever the 9-day moving average crosses over and closes above the 26-day moving average. By contrast, whenever the shorter-term moving average crosses over to close below the longer-term moving average, our trader would exit all long positions and initiate short positions.

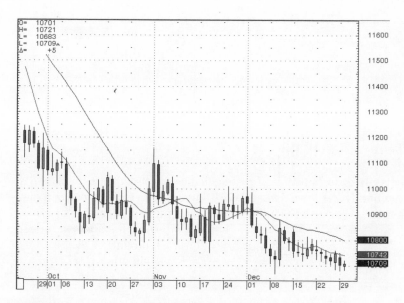

FIGURE 1.4 Spot dollar–yen with 9- and 26-day moving averages.

©2004 CQG, Inc. All rights reserved worldwide.

In contrast to trend-following indicators such as the two-moving average crossover, mathematical countertrend indicators, such as the relative
strength index (RSI) (see Figure 1.5), attempt to capitalize on the market's
tendency toward mean reversion (although mean reversion indicators can
be profitable in trending markets and vice versa).[14]

In 1978 Welles Wilder—who developed many commonly used mathematical technical indicators—developed the RSI to provide traders with an
objective tool for measuring when a market becomes either overbought or
oversold. The strength of the market is measured by this following for-
mula:

$$RSI = 100 - 100/1 + RS$$

$$\text{where} \quad RS = \frac{\text{Average of } X \text{ days when the market closed up}}{\text{Average of } X \text{ days when the market closed down}}$$

Fourteen periods—such as days or weeks—are most commonly used in
calculating the RSI. To determine the average "up" value, we add the total

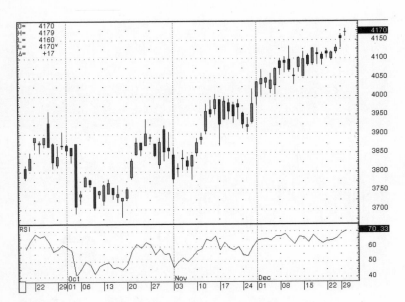

FIGURE 1.5   February 2004 Comex gold with RSI.

points gained on up days during the 14 days and divide that total by 14. To determine the average down value, we add the total points lost during the down days and divide that total by 14.[15] Most traders define a market as overbought when the RSI closes above 70 and oversold when the RSI closes below 30.

CHAPTER 2

Mathematical Technical Analysis

A Building Block for Mechanical Trading System Development

The general who wins a battle makes many calculations in his temple ere the battle is fought. The general who loses a battle makes but few calculations beforehand. Thus do many calculations lead to victory, and few calculations to defeat: how much more no calculation at all! It is by attention to this point that I can foresee who is likely to win or lose.

—Sun Tzu

Many excellent books on technical analysis provide readers with a comprehensive description of various mathematical technical indicators. This chapter does not attempt to duplicate their work but instead tries to address the essential facets of the most commonly employed indicators, including: an explanation of what the indicators are, why they work, and how they can provide system developers with ideal building blocks for mechanical trading systems.

Although I encourage readers to examine the various mathematical formulas behind these commonly employed indicators, I also freely admit that many traders successfully use these indicators without understanding the formulas on which they are based.

My choice of one indicator as opposed to another is almost exclusively dependent on that indicator's popularity at the time I wrote this book. Again, I focus on the most widely used indicators because the more market participants focus on a particular indicator, the more likely that it will be useful in system development. I usually favor using the default parameters designated by the indicator's developer. Thus, for example, mechanical trading systems shown based on Wilder's relative strength index (RSI) always use 9 or 14 periods.

Throughout this chapter I provide examples of indicators and trading systems that show profits. I could just as easily illustrate use of each indicator with losses, but I want to show why traders are drawn to a particular tool. Chapters 3, 4, and 5 discuss which technical indicators can be turned into successful trading systems. For now my goal is merely to explain what the most commonly used indicators are, why they are used, and how they form building blocks for comprehensive trading systems.

TYPES OF TECHNICAL INDICATORS

As stated in Chapter 1, there are two categories of mathematical technical indicators, those traditionally used to capitalize on the market's propensity toward mean reversion such as oscillators, and those that profit from trending price activity, such as moving averages. Although many books on technical analysis treat these various indicators as if they worked exclusively in either trend-following or mean-reverting trading environments, this book will show how indicators can be successfully applied to either realm.

Trend-Following Indicators: Why They Work

I have already highlighted some of the psychology behind the success of trend-following indicators in the discussion of reference points in behavioral finance. In Chapter 1, I showed how emphasis on reference price points led traders to take small profits and large losses. If we assume that the majority of market participants lack the psychological fortitude to allow profits to run and take losses quickly, then successful traders use trend-following indicators that necessarily reinforce their ability to actualize disciplined profit and loss goals. As a result, such trend-following technicians often find themselves on opposite sides of the market from their less successful counterparts. This theme of successful trading as the systematic "fading" (buying whenever the indicator would sell and vice versa) of unsuccessful traders will be revisited throughout the text.

Because successful trend-following traders are both utilizing trend-following indicators and acting contrary to mass psychology, we have shattered another myth of technical analysis, namely, that following the trend and contrarianism are mutually exclusive. Instead, contrary opinion is often the epitome of trend trading.

One of the best-known examples of trend-following contrarianism occurred in November 1982 when the Dow Jones Industrial Average (the

Dow) traded above 1,067.2 for first time in history. Traders buying that level were purchasing all-time new highs, which is in direct opposition to popular market wisdom admonishing us to buy low and sell high. Market participants focused solely on price reference points would have felt comfortable selling these historically "unsustainable" price levels. Therefore, the true contrarians were those following the trend and buying instead of selling these "high" prices. (The ultimate high of the market trend was not achieved until January 14, 2000, at 11,750 on the Dow).

By employing moving averages and other trend-following indicators, traders strive to attune themselves to the market's assessment of an asset's true value.

These indicators in turn help them to ignore psychological temptations inherent in fading what appears to be historically high or low prices. The success of trend-following indicators once again illustrates how the market rewards those who train themselves to do that which is unnatural and uncomfortable and punishes those desiring certainty, safety, and security.

Successful trend-following indicators not only force traders to abandon attempts to buy the bottom and sell the top, they reprogram traders away from destructive price reference points by forcing them to buy recent highs and sell recent lows.

Mean Reversion Indicators: Why They Work

If trend following is such a successful methodology, how can indicators based on the exact opposite philosophy generate consistent profits? The simple answer is that mean reversion indicators, such as RSI and other oscillators, work because they capitalize on the market's tendency to overextend itself.

Whether the trend has matured and is approaching climactic reversal or is still in its infancy and simply correcting a temporarily overbought or oversold condition, the market has an uncanny knack for separating the less experienced from their money by exploiting their greed, lack of patience, and complacency.

Imagine speculators who saw the bull move early but allowed fear of losses to prevent them from buying the market. As the trend matures, their anxiety and regret magnify in lockstep with forfeited profits until they finally capitulate and buy at any price so that they can participate in this once-in-a-lifetime trend. Since the thought process that accompanied their ultimate trading decision was purely emotional and devoid of price risk management considerations, when the inevitable pullback or change in trend occurs, greed and hysteria quickly shift to panic and capitulation.

Although mean reversion indicators such as oscillators attempt to somehow quantify these unsustainable levels of market emotionalism, they cannot do so as systematically as experienced traders with a "feel" for market psychology. For example, some on-floor traders are so attuned to the order flow entering their pit that they can consistently fade unsustainable emotionalism before it ever matures into a blip on a technician's radar.[1]

TREND-FOLLOWING INDICATORS: INDICATOR-DRIVEN TRIGGERS

Moving Averages

Simple Moving Averages and Popular Alternatives   In Chapter 1 we examined two indicator-driven triggers that are also complete mechanical trading systems: the single moving average and the two moving average crossover. The variations on moving average indicators are so numerous that a book could be devoted exclusively to their various flavors; however, in the interest of completeness, I address what I believe are some of the most significant alternatives to the simple moving average.

As discussed in Chapter 1, simple moving averages are the most widely used and the easiest to calculate because they give equal weighting to each data point within the data set. This issue of equal weighting to each data point leads technicians to seek alternatives to the simple moving average.

The problem with using a moving average that gives equal weight to each data point is that with longer-term moving averages—such as the 200-day moving average—the lagging aspect of indicator means it will be slower to respond to changes in trend. Obviously slower response times to trend changes could mean less reward and greater risk. One solution to the problem of the lagging nature of the simple moving average is to give greater weight to the most recent price action. Linearly weighted and exponentially smoothed moving averages both attempt to address the equal weighting issue by giving a larger weighting factor to more recent data.[2]

An alternative to the moving average weighting paradigm is found through the use of a volume-adjusted moving average. The volume-adjusted moving average suggests that directional movement accompanied by strong or weak volume is often a better measure of trend strength than any of the time-driven weighting models.

Another problem with moving averages is choosing between shorter and longer time parameters. The smaller the data set, such as a 7-day moving average, the quicker the indicator's ability to generate signals and the greater its reduction of lag time. But smaller data sets also result in more false trend-following signals during sideways, consolidation environments. As discussed, larger data sets, such as a 200-day moving average, will generate fewer, higher-quality entry signals, but those remaining signals will entail less reward and greater risk. Perry Kaufman, author of many books on technical analysis, with his adaptive moving average, attempts to address the issue of choosing between longer- and shorter-term moving averages by introducing a moving average that is attuned to market volatility, moving slower during periods of low volatility (i.e., sideways consolidation) and quicker in high-volatility or trending environments.[3]

Avoiding Whipsaws versus Improving Risk/Reward Everything in system development—as in life in general—is a trade-off. Our trade-off when working with moving averages is choosing between speeds of response to changes in trend and the number of false trend-following signals we are willing to endure.

Other solutions to this issue, besides the shorter- and longer-term moving averages, use of weighted moving averages, and the adaptive moving average, include the introduction of a second condition onto the moving average indicator in hopes of confirming valid signals and filtering out false breakouts. (False breakouts are also known as whipsaws because trend-following traders buying or selling on such signals get whipped into loss after loss until the market experiences a sustainable trend.) Although such confirmation patterns are limited only by the technician's imagination, the basic types of patterns are:

- Time-driven patterns, such as whipsaw waiting periods and modification of time horizons
- Percentage penetrations of the moving average
- The introduction of a second indicator or price-oriented trigger, such as the breaking of new highs or lows or the 10-period momentum indicator breaking above or below the zero level

Time-Driven Confirmation Patterns The concept of a whipsaw waiting period is fairly straightforward and simple. Instead of entry based on fulfillment of the indicator-driven trigger of settling above or below the moving average (as illustrated by Figure 2.1), now the indicator-driven trigger requires that the market not only settles above the moving average, but that it does so for a consecutive number of time periods (as shown in Figure 2.2).[4] *Note:* The trade results examined throughout this chapter just illustrate the different types of strategies employed. When we compare trading systems in later chapters, we will analyze the results on multiple asset classes with low to negative correlations to ensure the robustness of each system.

The other major flavor of time-driven patterns is that of modifying the time horizon employed, from 30-day to 30-minute moving averages. The premise behind changing the duration of moving averages is that when markets are trending, longer-term moving averages will be profitable. By contrast, shorter-term moving averages should prove more successful in

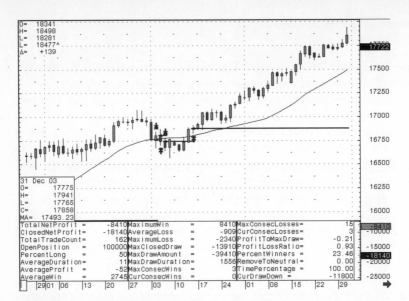

O=	18341			
H=	18498			
L=	18281			
L=	18477^			
Δ=	+139			

31 Dec 03
O= 17775
H= 17941
L= 17765
C= 17858
MA= 17493.23

TotalNetProfit =	-8410	MaximumWin =	8410	MaxConsecLosses= 15
ClosedNetProfit=	-18140	AverageLoss =	-909	CurConsecLosses= 3
TotalTradeCount=	162	MaximumLoss =	-2340	ProfitToMaxDraw= -0.21
OpenPosition =	100000	MaxClosedDraw =	-13910	ProfitLossRatio= 0.93
PercentLong =	50	MaxDrawAmount =	-39410	PercentWinners = 23.46
AverageDuration=	11	MaxDrawDuration=	1556	RemoveToNeutral = 0.00
AverageProfit =	-52	MaxConsecWins =	3	TimePercentage = 100.00
AverageWin =	2745	CurConsecWins =	0	CurDrawDown = -11800

FIGURE 2.1 Spot British pound–U.S. dollar with 26-day moving average as trigger—trade summary at bottom.

Note: All trade summaries include $100 round-turn trade deductions for slippage and commissions. ©2004 CQG, Inc. All rights reserved worldwide.

O=	18341			
H=	18498			
L=	18281			
L=	18477^			
Δ=	+139			

31 Dec 03
O= 17775
H= 17941
L= 17765
C= 17858
MA= 17493.23

TotalNetProfit =	2610	MaximumWin =	7710	MaxConsecLosses= 7
ClosedNetProfit=	-6660	AverageLoss =	-1711	CurConsecLosses= 1
TotalTradeCount=	70	MaximumLoss =	-4320	ProfitToMaxDraw= 0.09
OpenPosition =	100000	MaxClosedDraw =	-12180	ProfitLossRatio= 1.03
PercentLong =	50	MaxDrawAmount =	-29590	PercentWinners = 37.14
AverageDuration=	23	MaxDrawDuration=	1556	RemoveToNeutral = 0.00
AverageProfit =	37	MaxConsecWins =	5	TimePercentage = 99.94
AverageWin =	2995	CurConsecWins =	0	CurDrawDown = -120

FIGURE 2.2 Pound–U.S. dollar using 3-day whipsaw waiting period on a 26-day moving average trading system. Includes data from December 31, 1997, to December 31, 2003.

Note: All trade summaries include $100 round-turn trade deductions for slippage and commissions. ©2004 CQG, Inc. All rights reserved worldwide.

range-bound markets since 30- or 60-minute bar charts will have a higher probability of catching the short-term trend within the longer-term trading range (see Figures 2.3 and 2.4).

The assumption inherent in choosing longer- or shorter-term moving averages is the trader's ability to determine whether the market is a trending or mean reversion phase. This ability suggests either subjective judgment on the part of the trader or the introduction of an additional mathematical technical indicator, such as volatility or average directional movement index (ADX) to quantify the market's propensity to trend.[6]

Percentage Penetrations of the Moving Average   Another popular method of filtering out false signals generated by moving averages is the introduction of a percentage penetration prerequisite known as a moving average envelope. These envelopes are constructed by adding and subtracting a percentage of the moving average. Valid trading signals are generated when the market settles beyond the upper or lower envelopes of the moving average (see Figure 2.5).

Although moving average envelopes are traditionally used to filter out false trend-following signals, they also can be used as countertrend

FIGURE 2.3   February 2004 Nymex crude oil and 9- and 26-day crossover. Includes data from December 31, 1997, to December 31, 2003.

Note: All trade summaries include $100 round-turn trade deductions for slippage and commissions. ©2004 CQG, Inc. All rights reserved worldwide.

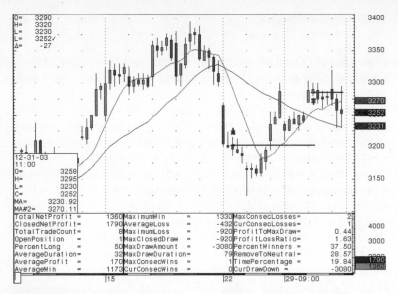

FIGURE 2.4 February 2004 Nymex crude oil using 60-minute bars and 9- and 26-period moving average crossovers. Includes data from December 31, 1997, to December 31, 2003.

Note: All trade summaries include $100 round-turn trade deductions for slippage and commissions. ©2004 CQG, Inc. All rights reserved worldwide.

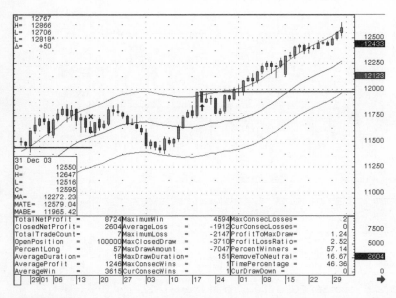

FIGURE 2.5 DM–euro–U.S. dollar with entry at 2.5% moving average envelope of a 21-day MA and exit at a 21-day MA. Includes data from December 31, 1997, to December 31, 2003.

Note: All trade summaries include $100 round-turn trade deductions for slippage and commissions. ©2004 CQG, Inc. All rights reserved worldwide.

indicators (see Figure 2.6). This concept of "fading" trend-following signals to capitalize on the market's propensity for mean reversion is a theme that we will revisit throughout the book. Although simply fading the moving average envelopes provides a method of generating entry signals, it does so without defining an exit method. Two distinct types of exits must be introduced to transform this indicator into a comprehensive trading system. First, we need to determine where we will exit the trade if mean reversion does occur as anticipated. Since our intention was to fade the envelopes, the obvious answer is exiting either at the moving average or with a percentage profit (i.e., 1 percent of the asset's value at entry).[7] The other, more critical exit criteria is the introduction of a fail-safe exit, which will prevent unlimited risk in the event that the market continues trending. Our fail-safe stop-loss level can be determined in numerous ways, such as the introduction of wider moving average envelopes or a percentage of the contract's value at the time of position entry.

Two and Three Moving Average Crossovers We have already examined two moving average crossover trading systems in some detail. The

FIGURE 2.6 Spot S&P 500 × 250 with fading of the 2.5% moving average envelope of a 21-day MA and profit targets of the MA or 1% of entry and 5% of entry price fail-safe stop loss. Includes data from December 31, 1997, to December 31, 2003.

Note: All trade summaries include $100 round-turn trade deductions for slippage and commissions. ©2004 CQG, Inc. All rights reserved worldwide.

Ichimoku Kinkou Hyou is similar to the traditional western moving average crossovers except that the moving average parameters are specifically set to 9 and 26 periods. Ichimoku also has a whipsaw waiting period built into it, as entry signals require not only that the 9 closes beyond the 26-period moving average, but also that the 26-period moving average starts moving in the direction of the crossover (compare Figures 2.7 and 2.8).

Jack Schwager, who writes extensively on technical analysis, incorporates this concept of following the momentum of the moving average by suggesting that traders can add to existing trend-following positions when the market's close violates the moving average. Although such violations traditionally trigger stop and reversals, Schwager argues that if the violation is not confirmed by a reversal of the moving average's trend, it offers traders a low-risk entry point.[8]

Except for moving average envelopes, so far the examination of the moving average has focused on stop-and-reverse trading systems, meaning that whenever conditions required the exiting of an open position, entry into an opposite position also was triggered. By contrast, the three moving average crossover system allows for neutrality (see Figure 2.9). Trade entry requires that the shortest moving average closes beyond the middle moving average and that the middle is beyond the longest. Whenever the shortest

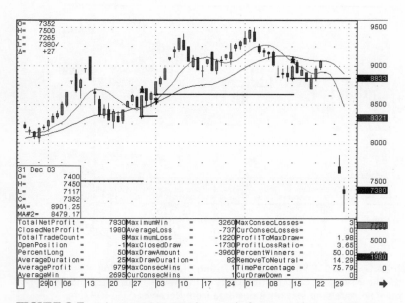

FIGURE 2.7 February 2004 CME live cattle futures with 9- and 26-day moving average crossover. Includes data from December 31, 1997, to December 31, 2003.

Note: All trade summaries include $100 round-turn trade deductions for slippage and commissions. ©2004 CQG, Inc. All rights reserved worldwide.

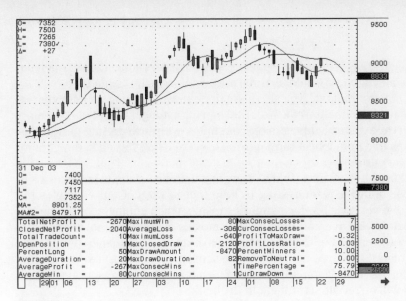

FIGURE 2.8 February 2004 CME live cattle futures with 2 moving average Ichimoku. Includes data from December 31, 1997, to December 31, 2003.

Note: All trade summaries include $100 round-turn trade deductions for slippage and commissions. ©2004 CQG, Inc. All rights reserved worldwide.

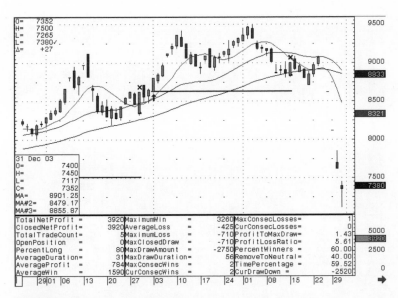

FIGURE 2.9 February 2004 CME live cattle futures with 9-, 26-, and 52-day moving average crossover system. Includes data from December 31, 1997, to December 31, 2003.

Note: All trade summaries include $100 round-turn trade deductions for slippage and commissions. ©2004 CQG, Inc. All rights reserved worldwide.

moving average is between the other two, it triggers liquidation of open positions and neutrality until all three are again correctly aligned.

Ichimoku Kinkou Hyou also has a three-moving-average version that includes the introduction of a 52-period moving average. As with its two-moving-average system, this version contains a whipsaw waiting period that requires that both longer-term moving averages have turned in direction of crossover prior to entry.

Although it is impossible to draw any definitive conclusion from a single case study, it is interesting to note that in both of our examples the Ichimoku versions produced inferior results when compared with the traditional moving average and the three moving average crossovers. In addition, both versions of the three moving average systems generated inferior track records when compared with the simpler, more robust two moving average crossovers (compare Figures 2.7 to 2.10). This concept of simple is better will be revisited throughout the book.

Other Indicator-Driven Trend Following Methods

Moving Average Convergence Divergence
The moving average convergence/divergence indicator—better known as the MACD—was devel-

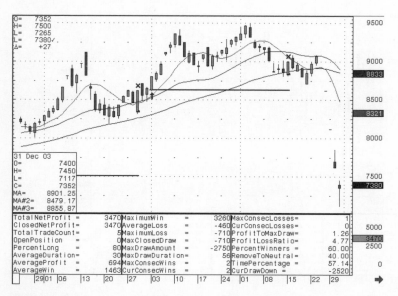

FIGURE 2.10 February CME live cattle futures with 3 moving average Ichimoku. Includes data from December 31, 1997, to December 31, 2003.

Note: All trade summaries include $100 round-turn trade deductions for slippage and commissions. ©2004 CQG, Inc. All rights reserved worldwide.

oped by Gerald Appel and is commonly used as a trend-following indicator that attempts to minimize trading range whipsaws. The MACD line is the numerical difference between a shorter-term, 13-period exponential moving average and a longer-term, 26-period exponential moving average. A third exponential moving average, known as the MACD's signal line, is a 9-period exponential average of the numerical difference between the 13- and 26-period exponential moving averages. MACD is commonly used as a trend-following stop and reverse trading system in which stop and reverse signals are generated whenever the MACD line closes beyond the MACD's signal line (see Figure 2.11).

Directional Movement Indicator and Average Directional Movement Index The directional movement indicator (DMI) is a trend-following indicator developed by Welles Wilder that attempts to measure market strength and direction. Instead of using the closing price for each period as an input, DMI uses each period's net directional movement. Net directional movement is defined as the largest part of a period's range that is outside of the previous period's range and includes separate calculations for positive movement (+DI) and negative movement (–DI).[9]

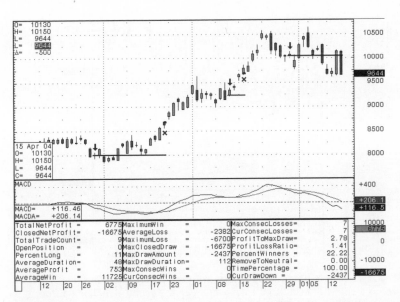

FIGURE 2.11 July 2004 CBOT soybeans with MACD crossover. Includes data from April 7, 2003, to April 15, 2004.

Note: All trade summaries include $100 round-turn trade deductions for slippage and commissions. ©2004 CQG, Inc. All rights reserved worldwide.

If the +DI is greater than the –DI, then the market is said to be trending higher; if –DI is greater than the +DI, then the indicator suggests a bearish trend. Because market direction is determined by whether DMI is above or below the zero line, it is another stop and reverse trend-following system (see Figure 2.12).

The average directional movement index, or ADX, is an index of the relative strength of the market's trend. It is derived by applying a 9-period smoothing of the result of dividing the difference between the absolute value of +DI and DI by the sum of +DI and DI. If the resulting percentage is above 20, the market is viewed as trending, whereas readings below 20 suggest sideways activity (see Figure 2.13).

When comparing Figures 2.12 and 2.13, it is interesting to note that inclusion of ADX resulted in inferior system performance. Although it is impossible to draw conclusions from a single example, I offer it to readers here as a caution flag. Just because data vendors or indicator developers link two studies together does not necessarily mean their combination will increase profitability.

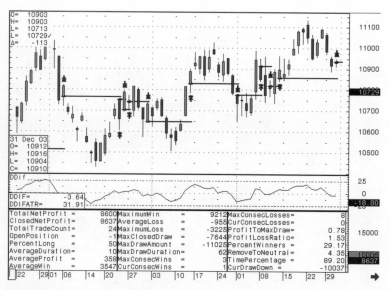

FIGURE 2.12 March 2004 CBOT T-bonds with the difference between +DI and –DI shown as a single line and DMI crossover system. Results include data from December 31, 2002, to December 31, 2003.

Note: All trade summaries include $100 round-turn trade deductions for slippage and commissions. ©2004 CQG, Inc. All rights reserved worldwide.

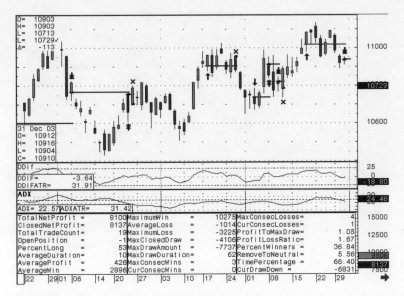

FIGURE 2.13 March 2004 CBOT T-bonds with DMI crossover system and ADX filter Results include data from December 31, 2002, to December 31, 2003.

Note: All trade summaries include $100 round-turn trade deductions for slippage and commissions. ©2004 CQG, Inc. All rights reserved worldwide.

Parabolic The final indicator-driven triggered trend-following method that we will examine is Wilder's parabolic, or stop and reverse (SAR). This is another trend-following system that is always in the market and whose stop-and-reverse trigger points take on a parabolic shape as the trend matures. The parabolic curve of the stop and reverse levels is achieved through the indicator's incorporation of an acceleration factor.[10]

The key to success with parabolic lies in the ability to determine whether the market is in a sustainable trending environment. Chapter 3 examines these issues in more detail; for now, suffice it to say that specific asset classes display a greater propensity to trend. Unless a trader's superior grasp of fundamentals suggests a high probability of a sustainable trend, Wilder's parabolic probably should be used with such vehicles (see Figure 2.14).

If SAR performs poorly in many markets, it seems logical to fade its stop and reverse signals, as we did in our work with moving average envelopes. To review, we successfully transformed the moving average envelopes from a trend-following system into a mean reversion system by fading all trading signals generated and adding a fail-safe exit to prevent unlimited risk in the event that the market continued trending.

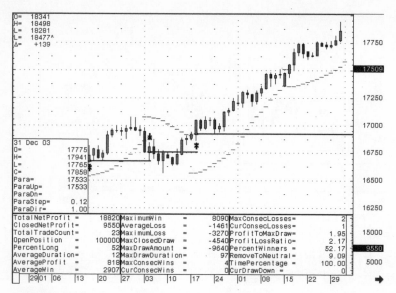

FIGURE 2.14 Spot pound/U.S. dollar with parabolic. Includes data from December 31, 2002, to December 31, 2003.

Note: All trade summaries include $100 round-turn trade deductions for slippage and commissions. ©2004 CQG, Inc. All rights reserved worldwide.

In this instance we made the fail-safe stop loss 2.5 standard deviations from the 20-day moving average and stated that all entries required the market to be trading at less than 2.5 standard deviations from the 20-day moving average (see Figure 2.15).

PRICE-TRIGGERED TREND-FOLLOWING INDICATORS: DONCHIAN'S CHANNEL BREAKOUT

Richard Donchian's nth period or channel breakout system is not only a price-triggered trend-following indicator, but also a comprehensive stop and reverse trading system. Trading signals are generated whenever the market price is equal to or greater than the highest high or the lowest low of the past n periods (Donchian used 20 days).[11]

The reason this simple trading system is so successful is that it capitalizes on one of the primary psychological flaws of novice traders: their desire to buy bottoms and sell tops. Because channel breakout only buys or sells when a trend is already established, its entry and reversal points tend

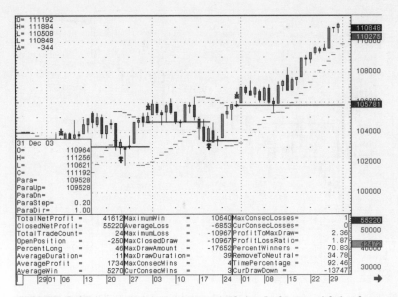

FIGURE 2.15 Cash S&P 500 × 250 with "fading" of SAR and fail-safe stop at 2.5 standard deviations beyond the 20-day moving average. Results include data from December 31, 2002, to December 31, 2003.

Note: All trade summaries include $100 round-turn trade deductions for slippage and commissions. ©2004 CQG, Inc. All rights reserved worldwide.

to gravitate to key horizontal support or resistance levels. As the trend matures, capitulation of those seeking reversal adds to the system's profitability (see Figure 2.16).

MEAN REVERSION INDICATOR-DRIVEN TRIGGERS: OSCILLATORS

All of the most commonly employed mean reversion indicators are oscillators. The most popular oscillators can be categorized as percentage, differential, or statistical oscillators. In all instances the goal in using oscillators is to fade a temporarily unsustainable level of market emotionalism in hopes of mean reversion. Although a mathematical technical indicator may not be able to quantify extreme emotionalism with same the consistency as an experienced trader, as long as an oscillator can be linked to a solid risk quantification mechanism, it may prove a useful tool in the trader's arsenal.

FIGURE 2.16 June 2004 IMM eurodollar with 20-day channel breakout. Results include data from December 31, 2002, to December 31, 2003.

Note: All trade summaries include $100 round-turn trade deductions for slippage and commissions. ©2004 CQG, Inc. All rights reserved worldwide.

Percentage Oscillators

Stochastics Stochastics was developed by George Lane and is based on the principle that as a market reaches temporarily unsustainable extremes, daily closing prices tend to be closer to the upper (overbought) or lower (oversold) end of each day's range. As a market loses momentum, closing prices tend to reverse these trends.

Fast %K or %K measures, on a percentage basis, where the latest closing price is in relation to the total price range over a specific period of days (9 and 14 days are the most commonly used default values). Fast %K is used in calculation of fast stochastics. The more popular slow stochastics is generated by calculating Slow %K (SK), which is a 3-day moving average of Fast %K and Slow %D (SD), which is a 3-day moving average of slow %K (SK).

Either version produces two lines that are charted on a 0 to 100 scale. Traditionally, buy and sell signals are generated when the slow %K line crosses over the Slow %D line in overbought or oversold territory. Overbought is usually defined as somewhere between 70 and 80, with oversold readings between 30 and 20. Although it is possible to develop a moderately successful trading system using the SK-SD crossover, my slow stochastics extremes trading system offers a simpler alternative.

The 14-day stochastics extremes generate buy signals whenever SD closes below 15 and sell signals when SD closes above 85. As with the fading of trend-following indicators, such as moving average envelopes and parabolics, to transform this mean reversion indicator into a comprehensive trading system, rules for exiting with profits and with losses are needed. For profitable exits, we will use SD closes above 30 and below 70, and our fail-safe exit will be designated as 2.5 percent of the asset's value at time of entry (see Figure 2.17).

Relative Strength Index   Chapter 1 highlighted RSI as a mean reversion indicator because it is among the most popular and well-known of the oscillators. Like stochastics, the RSI is plotted on a 0 to 100 scale, with the 70/30 combination as the most widely used overbought/oversold boundary parameters. As with stochastics, the most popular time periods are the 9- and 14-day versions. Traditionally, RSI generates entry signals whenever the index extends into overbought or oversold territory then falls below the upper boundary or rises above the lower boundary.

Since stochastics and RSI are so similar, the most obvious choice for development of a mean reversion trading system is use of the same logic as

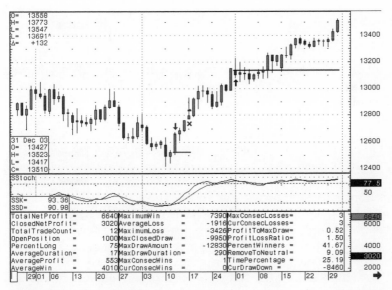

FIGURE 2.17   Spot euro/yen with sloc stochastics extremes trading system. Data shows results from December 31, 2000, to December 31, 2003.

Note: All trade summaries include $100 round-turn trade deductions for slippage and commissions. ©2004 CQG, Inc. All rights reserved worldwide.

illustrated in the stochastics extremes trading system. As a result, the 14-day RSI extremes trading system (see Figure 2.18) enters trades whenever the indicator closes beyond either 70 or 30. Exiting with profits occurs whenever RSI closes above 35 or below 65. The system utilizes the same 2.5 percent failsafe stop that was employed in stochastics extremes.

Differential Oscillators   We have already examined several differential oscillators, including the two-moving average, the DMI, and the MACD differential oscillator. As stated, differential oscillators are based on the difference between two data series. In contrast to percentage oscillators, which range from 0 to 100, differential oscillators have no numerical limit and so determination of overbought or oversold levels is problematic. Most technicians view these oscillators as mean reversion indicators, because they lack absolute numerical ceilings or floors. So far I have used differential oscillators only in developing trend-following systems based on the indicator crossing beyond the zero line.

Momentum and Rate of Change   The momentum and the rate of change (ROC) oscillators produce remarkably similar results because they both measure the closing price of x periods ago (10 periods is the most com-

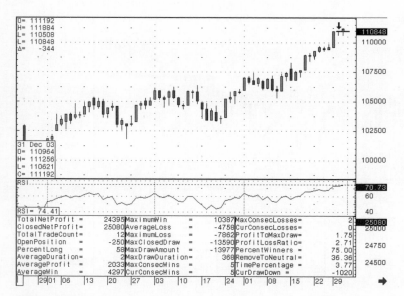

FIGURE 2.18   Cash S&P 500 × 250 using RSI extremes trading system. Data show results from December 31, 1997, to December 31, 2003.

Note: All trade summaries include $100 round-turn trade deductions for slippage and commissions. ©2004 CQG, Inc. All rights reserved worldwide.

monly employed default value for these indicators) in relation to the latest closing price. (Momentum subtracts, whereas ROC divides closing price of x periods ago by the latest closing price.) If the latest closing price is above the closing price x periods ago, the oscillator is positive, if it is below the closing price x periods ago, the oscillator is negative. Subsequently, these oscillators are tailor made for a stop and reverse trend-following trading system with buy and sell signals triggered by closing beyond the zero level.

A comparison of Figures 2.19 and 2.20 shows that these systems often produce identical results and that utilization of both systems offers little benefit in terms of system diversification.

Statistical Oscillators   Statistical oscillators are based on a statistical measurement known as the standard deviation (a mathematical measure of how widely dispersed a data set is from its mean). Instead of comparing current prices to past prices on a relative percentage basis, statistical oscillators compare current prices to a statistically measured amount of past price movement (deviation from the data set's mean). These oscillators use the standard deviation of past prices over a specific period as the benchmark for "normal" price movement, and then compare the current price to the benchmark of normal price movement to measure the momentum of the

FIGURE 2.19 Spot Australian dollar/U.S. dollar with 10-day momentum. Includes data from December 31, 2002, to December 31, 2003.

Note: All trade summaries include $100 round-turn trade deductions for slippage and commissions. ©2004 CQG, Inc. All rights reserved worldwide.

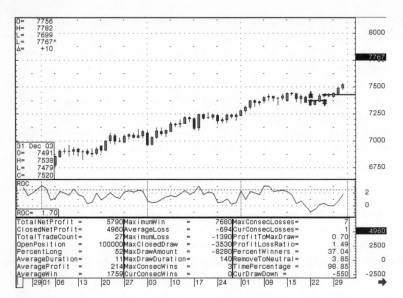

FIGURE 2.20 Spot Australian dollar/U.S. dollar with 10-day ROC. Includes data from December 31, 2002, to December 31, 2003.

Note: All trade summaries include $100 round-turn trade deductions for slippage and commissions. ©2004 CQG, Inc. All rights reserved worldwide.

market. The benefit of this approach is that the standard to which current prices are compared changes in response to shifts in market volatility.

Bollinger Bands Bollinger bands, which were popularized by John Bollinger, who started as a market technician on CNBC, are constructed by calculating the standard deviation of prices over a specified period of time (Bollinger used 20 periods as his default value) and then adding and subtracting two standard deviations to a simple 20-period moving average. By constantly recalculating the standard deviation of recent prices, the indicator remains attuned to changes in market volatility since overbought and oversold levels will be harder to reach in a volatile market and easier to achieve in quiet markets.

Because Bollinger bands are based on two standard deviations from the 20-day moving average, they should theoretically encompass around 97 percent of all price action. When the market closes beyond the upper or lower bands, such price action is traditionally viewed as unsustainable. In fact, this often proves to be the case, and Bollinger bands are a commonly used as a building block in mean reversion trading systems (see Figure 2.21).

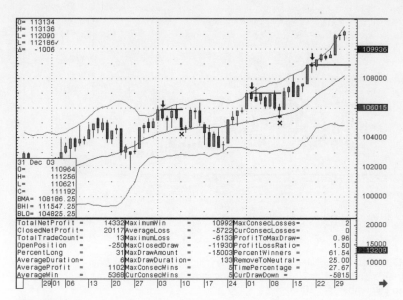

FIGURE 2.21 Cash S&P 500 × 250 with entry at upper and lower bands and exits at 20-day moving average or at 2.5% fail-safe stop loss. Includes data from December 31, 2002, to December 31, 2003.

Note: All trade summaries include $100 round-turn trade deductions for slippage and commissions. ©2004 CQG, Inc. All rights reserved worldwide.

If moving average envelopes and Wilder's parabolic—trend-following indicators—were used to develop countertrend systems, then logic suggests that percentage penetration indicators—such as Bollinger bands—mean reversion tools would be valuable in building trend-following systems. In fact, the breaking of the upper or lower bands can signal the onset of a powerful and sustainable trend, as illustrated by Figure 2.22.

Commodity Channel Index The commodity channel index (CCI) examines today's price in relation to a moving average (usually 20 periods), then divides this by the mean deviation of prices multiplied by .015.[12] Although Donald Lambert, the developer of the CCI, originally intended the oscillator to be used as a trend-following indicator, with a buy signal generated on an initial reading greater than +100 and a sell signal generated on an initial reading of −100 (see Figure 2.23), currently it is most commonly used as a mean reversion indicator. Technicians disagree as to what numbers constitute an unsustainable level for the indicator. Some interpret levels greater than +100 and less than −100 as overbought and oversold, whereas others require readings greater than +200 or less than −200 prior to fading the trend in hope of mean reversion (see Figure 2.24).

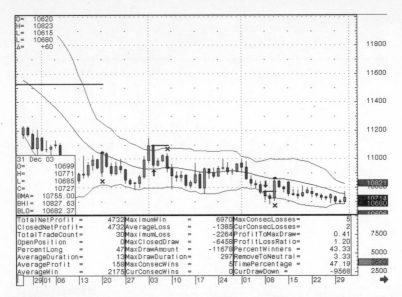

FIGURE 2.22 U.S. dollar/yen with entries triggered by closes beyond upper and lower bands and exits at 20-day moving average. Includes data from December 31, 2000, to December 31, 2003.

Note: All trade summaries include $100 round-turn trade deductions for slippage and commissions. ©2004 CQG, Inc. All rights reserved worldwide.

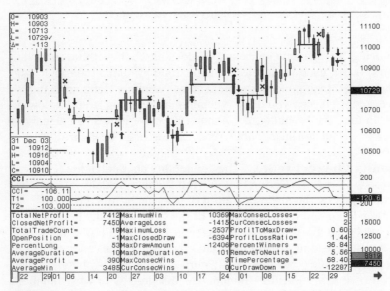

FIGURE 2.23 March 2004 CBOT U.S. T-bonds with CCI trading system based on entry triggers of closing at or beyond +100/−100 and exits at 0 or better. Includes data from December 31, 2002, to December 31, 2003.

Note: All trade summaries include $100 round-turn trade deductions for slippage and commissions. ©2004 CQG, Inc. All rights reserved worldwide.

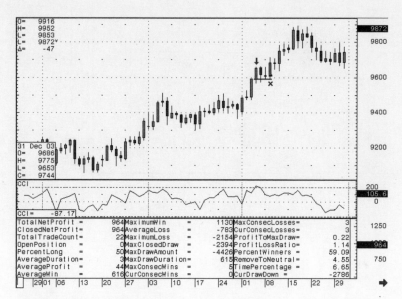

```
O=    9916
H=    9952
L=    9853
L=    9872ᵛ                                                              9872
Δ=     -47                                                               9800


                                                                        9600


                                                                        9400


 31 Dec 03                                                              9200
 O=   9686
 H=   9775
 L=   9653
 C=   9744

 CCI                                                                     200
                                                                        105.6
                                                                          0
 CCI =     -87.17
 TotalNetProfit  =        964 MaximumWin     =       1130 MaxConsecLosses=      3   1250
 ClosedNetProfit=        964 AverageLoss     =       -783 CurConsecLosses=      3
 TotalTradeCount=         22 MaximumLoss     =      -2154 ProfitToMaxDraw=   0.22
 OpenPosition   =          0 MaxClosedDraw   =      -2394 ProfitLossRatio=   1.14    964
 PercentLong    =         50 MaxDrawAmount   =      -4426 PercentWinners =  59.09
 AverageDuration=          3 MaxDrawDuration =        615 RemoveToNeutral=   4.55    750
 AverageProfit  =         44 MaxConsecWins   =          5 TimePercentage =   6.65
 AverageWin     =        616 CurConsecWins   =          0 CurDrawDown    =  -2786
       29 01  06    13    20   27    03   10    17    24   01   08    15    22    29
```

FIGURE 2.24 Australian dollar/Canadian dollar with CCI using –200 and +200 levels as entry triggers and –100 or +100 as exits with fail-safe stop exit at 2.5%. Includes data from December 31, 2000, to December 31, 2003.

Note: All trade summaries include $100 round-turn trade deductions for slippage and commissions. ©2004 CQG, Inc. All rights reserved worldwide.

CHAPTER 3

Trend-Following Systems

A Matter of Fortitude

Patience and fortitude conquer all things.

—Ralph Waldo Emerson

This chapter and the next two address trading systems tailored toward the three basic trader personality types: trend-following, mean-reversion, and day-trading personalities. Although there are infinite gradations within each of these categories, years of empirical observation have led me to believe that all traders display a natural inclination to gravitate to one of these three basic psychological profiles.

This chapter examines in detail the profitability and robustness of various trend-following systems outlined in Chapter 2. A cursory examination of the trend-following system examples in that chapter clues us in to two traits necessary for successful trend traders: patience and fortitude. Although it is tempting to merely gloss over the other statistics and focus on the total net profit column, we really need to search our innermost selves and ask such questions as: Am I prepared to stick with this trading technique after suffering seven consecutive losing trades? and Can I make my peace with enduring twice as many losing as profitable trades?

Few who embark on the path of system trading ever ask themselves these questions beforehand. And yet they are obviously the most important issues for the trend trader to address. This is why in the book's preface I emphasized that the development of a successful trading system is almost beside the point. Given enough time and the right software, almost anyone can develop a profitable system, but is it the right system for their trading personality? Do people who want to be trend traders have the discipline, patience, and price risk management skills needed to stick with that system after experiencing its seventh consecutive losing trade? If not, then they might not have the personality traits needed for successful trend trading. This is not to say that every trend trader will suffer through seven consecutive losses; however, people who adopt trend-following strategies should be psychologically prepared for this occurrence as a distinct possibility.

I hope by now that I have shattered any illusion readers might have that using mechanical trading systems will make life as a trader easier. As long as such illusions persist, the discipline and patience required to pursue profitable trading will be sabotaged, for successful trading requires a reprogramming of the trader, a transformation of expectations and an acceptance of the limitations and drawbacks inherent in almost any robust trading methodology.

PRELIMINARY CONSIDERATIONS

Chapter 2 addressed the issue of how indicators could be turned into trading systems; it did not cover the process of system development and various considerations inherent in the backtesting of a trading strategy. Now that we are ready to analyze the success or failure of a particular trading system, we need to examine these issues.

Considerations with Any Indicator-Driven Triggers

Entry and exit levels are self-explanatory for price-driven triggers since the violation of a historical high or low signals entry or exit of a particular price-driven trading system, such as channel breakout. By contrast, indicator-driven triggers raise a myriad of entry and exit level questions for system developers. The first question is fairly subjective: Are we as traders able to watch the screen and place entry or exit orders as the indicator levels are violated intraday? If so, we run the risk of trading an intraday violation that could reverse itself and not trigger a signal at end of day. Of course, the advantage in taking an intraday signal is the potential for better prices (less risk and greater reward); however, most system developers prefer knowing that the signal will remain valid at end of day (since the results of all intermediate to long-term trading system are necessarily based on end-of-day signals only).

Because most system developers rely on end-of-day indicator-driven entry and exit triggers, the next question is: Do we assume our entry/exit price level to be the close or the following day's open? Although either of these alternatives is acceptable in most instances, in choosing entry on the close, we run the risk of the indicator trading just beyond the trigger level in the final minute of trading and then settling back to levels that would not generate a signal. This is not usually as severe of a problem as taking intra-day signals because, for most markets (especially 24-hour ones), the price level for the following day's open usually will be fairly close to our entry price. Nevertheless, the only surefire method of avoiding false entry and exit signals is to set the indicator trigger to the close (or settlement price) and the entry or exit level to the opening price of the following day.

Composition of Portfolios   In determining the success of a particular trading system, ideally we would like to test our results on as many assets as possible. Unfortunately, many of these assets are highly correlated with each other. Inclusion of too many highly correlated assets (e.g., soybeans, corn, soybean meal, Chicago wheat, Kansas City wheat, soybean oil, Minneapolis wheat, and rough rice) could skew the backtested results of the system, leading us to believe either that a profitable system loses money or, more important, that a losing system is profitable.

Next we must make some assumptions regarding slippage and commissions that are both realistic and conservative. For example, it is unrealistic to assume that our stop price and our fill price will be identical. Because we will be forced to make assumptions regarding "reasonable" slippage and commission levels on our backtested portfolio, we want to ensure that these assumptions are conservative enough to have a high probability of replication when trading the system in real time. As a result, ideally our portfolio should contain only those assets that experience minimal slippage, in other words, those that are the most liquid. It is for this reason that low-liquidity instruments such as Nymex coal futures are not included in our portfolio. (Note that the liquidity of various assets changes over time. As a result, traders are strongly encouraged to monitor volume and open interest statistics provided by the various exchanges.)

Finally, if the market chosen for our backtesting produces consistent profits, but those profits are so small—due to either lack of volatility or value of contract—that commissions and slippage turn those paper profits into net losers, then those markets should be omitted. It is for this reason that I have chosen not to include Chicago Board of Trade (CBOT) corn in my backtested portfolio despite its excellent liquidity.

The other issue to consider regarding contract size is that just as we avoided inclusion of highly correlated assets in our portfolio to ensure the robustness of the system, as much as possible we should ensure that no single market within our portfolio has a contract size that dwarfs or enlarges the weighting of other portfolio components. It is for this reason that I have chosen the E-mini S&P 500 futures contract instead of the full-sized S&P 500 futures contract. Finally, many system developers include weighting matrices to address these issues. Although my portfolio does not employ such a matrix, readers are strongly encouraged to experiment with various weightings to achieve portfolio component parity.

With these considerations in mind, I have chosen to include one asset from the asset classes shown in Table 3.1.

Data Integrity: Expiration of Futures Contracts

The figures provided in Chapter 2 were either cash market charts, such as spot Interbank foreign exchange (Forex) or cash S&P 500 index, or they were futures contracts for a specific delivery month. This was fine for showcasing how specific technical indicators can be transformed into trading systems, but to generate 10 years of backtested results for a particular trading system on a portfolio, we need to address the issue of expiration of futures contracts.

Nearest Futures Charts   The traditional method of dealing with expiration of futures contracts is known as linked nearest contract or nearest futures charting. The nearest futures chart is constructed by including the data history of the futures contract closest to expiration. Following the front month contract's expiration, the chart begins displaying the price history of the new nearest futures contract.

The problem with these charts is that there are usually significant dif-

TABLE 3.1   Composition of backtested portfolio.

Asset Class	Asset[a]	Asset Symbol
Equity Indices	CME E-Mini S&P 500[b]	ES
Mid/Long-Term Rates	CBOT Treasury notes	TY
Short-Term Rates	CME eurodollars	ED
European Currencies	IMM Swiss franc[c]	SF
Asian Currencies	IMM Japanese yen	JY
Energy	Nymex crude oil	CL
Metals	Comex gold	GC
Grains	CBOT soybeans	S
Meats	CME lean hogs	LH
Food & Fibers	NYBOT cotton	CT

[a]To ensure uniformity, all assets shown are day session only.

[b]Cash S&P 500 Index x 50 was used to simulate CME E-mini S&P futures.

[c]Due the shift from D marks to euros during the backtested period, IMM Swiss francs were used for European currencies.

Data source: CQG, Inc.

ferences between the expiring contract's final price and the initial price recorded for the new front month contract. This divergence between the two data sets could result in huge price gaps and, more important, for our purposes, false trading signals. For example, by comparing Figures 3.1 and 3.2, if the February lean hogs contract expired today, the nearest futures chart would rise by 332 points, probably triggering false trading signals in most intermediate-term trading systems.

Equalized Continuation Price Series Charts   Most high-functionality data providers enable their subscribers to overcome this problem of false trading signals on long-term nearest futures charts by providing equalized continuation or point-based back-adjusted data series charting. With an equalized continuation series chart, the problem of contract rollover is resolved by the trader choosing a specific number of days prior to expiration day as the trigger for rolling the data in the chart back to the older futures contract month's data series.

Returning to the lean hogs contract rollover problem, if in March 2004 we were to backtest a particular trading system for lean hogs using a equalized continuation price series chart with a designated rollover date of January 19, 2004, as of that date our chart would begin to reflect February 2004

FIGURE 3.1   February 2004 CME lean hogs futures.

FIGURE 3.2   April 2004 CME lean hogs futures.

data plus the 332-point differential between the February and April contracts. This is because on our designated rollover date the prices were:

February 2004 lean hogs = $5,475

April 2004 lean hogs = $5,807

Our continuous chart would add 332 to all February lean hogs data on and prior to the designated contract rollover date.[1]

Although equalized continuation charts are a tremendous improvement over nearest futures charts for data integrity in system backtesting, they are not without drawbacks. The first and most obvious problem is that the numbers displayed on these charts are derived through an artificial adjustment of prices, and so the price levels shown are worthless in terms of determining horizontal and trend-line support and resistance and retracement level.

Another problem with equalized continuation charting is that the process of deriving equivalent historical prices often leads to data within the series containing prices of zero or negative numbers. This prohibits our use of stop-loss levels based on a percentage of the contract's value at time of entry. Although we could always refer back to the actual historical prices at the time of entry to derive a percentage-based stop-loss level, there is no need to bother as there are a plethora of equally robust mechanisms for stop-loss placement that can be employed instead.

Point Value versus Percentage Changes in Data History A final issue applies not only to equalized continuation charts, but also to all of historical data. This is the problem of point value changes as opposed to percentage value changes. I will use equalized continuation charts to exemplify the issue. Equalized continuation charts merely adjust the price difference between today's data and historical data, as illustrated by the lean hog example. In many instances, if the asset in question has experienced a long-term bull market trend, then the price differences between entry and exit will be dramatically different from the percentage differences.

For example, let us assume that our equalized continuation chart for Nymex natural gas futures shows a long entry price of $1.001 during August 1991 and an exit price of $1.356 for a profit of $3,450.00 per contract (trade profit was $3,550.00 minus $100.00 for slippage and commissions). Although the absolute price difference between entry and exit levels is correct, if we consider this difference in percentage terms based on August 1991 valuations, we can determine that the actual contract was trading at $1.50 and that a price move of $0.355 represents a 23.67% profit. Now compare this same price move based on October 2003 natural gas prices of $6.00 and our 23.67% profit shrinks to a mere 5.92%.

Thomas Stridsman's book on trading systems addresses these issues in great detail and offers solutions regarding this flaw in equalized continuation data histories. Readers who feel that their backtested results will be affected by such limitations are encouraged to adopt his solutions. In other words, if data are based solely on trading a market with a historical trend similar to the natural gas example, then use percentage instead of price changes.[2] However, in pursuing this methodology, remember that the exchange can change the point value of its contracts. Blindly applying a percentage change without consideration of this fact (and of how the software vendor handles such changes) can skew results as dramatically as sticking with the originally flawed price change calculations.[3]

Examples of other instances in which application of percentage as opposed to price changes would be questionable are the foreign exchange and fixed income markets. Because foreign exchange price increases or decreases are totally dependent on the base currency chosen for valuation, the application of percentage changes are subjective and misleading. This is illustrated by the International Money Market (IMM) Japanese yen contract, which was trading around .003400 in December 1976 and .009200 in

November 2003. Based on these price comparisons, we might erroneously assume that greater weighting should be given to trades executed in 1976 since equal price moves would represent a greater percentage change. This is obviously not the case since the IMM valuation is in Japanese yen–U.S. dollar and use of the interbank market valuations of 298 in 1976 and 109 in 2003 (which are expressed in U.S. dollar–Japanese yen terms) would suggest the exact opposite percentage weightings.

Applying percentage as opposed to price changes to the fixed income market implies a less severe but equally flawed assumption regarding the data. This is due to the inverse relationship between price and yield.[4] If an assumption is to be made regarding the application of percentage changes to the fixed income markets, it should be that as prices increase, they may represent lower volatility and therefore would entail a reduced percentage weighting vis-à-vis today's data.

Despite the flaws just detailed, in light of the nature and historical trends of the assets contained with my model portfolio, I remain reasonably comfortable with using equalized continuation charts and have chosen to set the rollover date to 20 days prior to expiration of the contract. Nevertheless, in some instances, where the liquidity was adequate and the correlations between the spot and futures market for a specific asset were significantly high enough, I have decided to use the spot market's data history.

Backtested Portfolio Results   Another practical limitation in the presentation of historically backtested results on any significant sampling (for intermediate to long-term systems, 10 to 30 years of historical data are considered a statistically significant data sampling) is the problem of estimating worst peak-to-valley equity drawdowns. To accurately calculate the worst peak-to-valley drawdown on a daily basis, we would need to track daily mark to markets on all assets within the portfolio for the entire data history in question. At the time of this writing, most data vendors with system development and backtesting capabilities do not offer backtested results for a portfolio of assets. Consequently, all worst drawdown and maximum consecutive loss numbers shown in the portfolio totals columns in this and the next chapters are derived from profit/loss and win/loss as of trade exit dates.

Explanation of the Portfolio Results Tables

For the asset symbol definitions, refer back to Table 3.1. Although I could have chosen to employ all 24 of the fields used in CQG's backtested performance results, I have chosen to highlight 10 fields that I feel are most essential in evaluation of a system's robustness:

1. *Total net profit* examines profitability irrespective of risk taken to achieve these results. Because of this limitation, other measures included in our backtested results are superior analytical tools. However, this number is useful because it allows us to quickly add and compare various portfolio component results for numerous systems without additional calculations.

2. *Number of trades (# Trades)* shows the total number of trades taken during the backtested period. For trend-following systems, we want this number to be as low as possible without sacrificing profitability.

3. *Number of days (# Days)* shows the average duration of a trade. As with number of trades, all else being equal, the lower the number of days in a trade while still generating superior results the better.

   The only caveat here is whether the system is trend following or mean reverting. If it is trend following, then the higher number of days in the trade will usually result in larger profits.

4. *Maximum drawdown amount (Max Draw)* tells us the maximum peak-to-valley equity drawdown during the backtested period. This number defines our absolute minimum capitalization requirements to trade the system. (Although prudent money management suggests allowance for at least 50 percent beyond our worst historical drawdown; see Chapter 8 for more details.)

   Most system developers also include the "maximum loss" column in their performance analysis tables. Maximum loss tells us the largest loss experienced on a per-trade basis. Although prudent price risk management suggests that our maximum loss on a per trade basis should not exceed 1 to 2 percent of total account equity, this measure does not consider correlations within a portfolio (see Chapter 8).

   Because one of the main precepts of this book is reduction of risk through diversification among negatively and/or uncorrelated asset classes (see Chapter 9), I feel that the maximum loss experienced on a per-trade basis can be a somewhat misleading and therefore an inferior measure when compared with that of maximum peak to valley equity drawdown. If, for whatever reason (e.g., lack of capital, corporate prohibitions, etc.), a diversified portfolio of assets cannot be traded, inclusion of the maximum loss measure and adherence to the 1 to 2 percent rule becomes an absolute necessity.

5. *Maximum drawdown duration (MDD)* is the longest duration of a drawdown in equity prior to the achievement of a new equity peak. This number is essential in psychologically preparing us for how long we must wait to experience a new peak in account equity.

6. *Maximum consecutive losses (MCL)* is the maximum number of

consecutive losses endured throughout the backtested period. Just as MDD is important in dispelling any fantasies regarding a system's ability to jump continuously from equity peak to ever higher peaks, MCL shows ahead of time exactly how many consecutive losses successful trend traders would have endured to enjoy the system's total net profit.

7. *Profit to maximum drawdown (P:MD)* refers to the average profit to maximum drawdown ratio. The higher this ratio is, the better. This is probably the most important field listed because it allows us to examine profit in relation to risk endured to achieve that profitability.

8. *Profit loss ratio (P:L ratio)* refers to the average profit to average loss ratio. As with P:MD, the higher these numbers are, the better. Trend-following systems should have very good P:L ratios because they generally display a low winning percentage of trades. This means that large profits and small losses are key in generating a good P:MD ratio. These ratios will drop for mean reversion systems, but the winning percentage of trades should compensate for this.

9. *Percent winners (% W)* is the percentage of winning trades. As stated, trend systems generally will have relatively low %Ws and mean reversion systems typically display high %Ws.

10. *Time percentage (Time %)* refers to the amount of time that this system has an open position in the market. If all other fields were equal, then a lower time percentage would be preferable because it means our available capital is tied up for less time to yield the same rate of return.

Trading System Parameters: Less Is More

All of the trading systems examined herein are the simplest imaginable while still showing overall profitability. I argue that simple is better because trading systems with the fewest parameters have the best overall chance at generating future results that are similar to their past performance history.

TWO MOVING AVERAGE CROSSOVER

The two moving average crossover is probably the simplest and most robust trend-following trading system. Traders initiate long positions and exit shorts whenever the shorter-term moving average settles above the longer-term moving average; they stop and reverse whenever the shorter-term moving average settles below the longer-term moving average.

Using CQG, the programming code for a typical two moving average crossover system is written in this way:

Long Entry and Short Exit:

MA(@,Sim,9)[-1] XABOVE MA(@,Sim,26)[-1]

Short Entry and Long Exit:

MA(@,Sim,9)[-1] XBELOW MA(@,Sim,26)[-1]

Table 3.2 presents the backtested portfolio results from December 31, 1992, to December 31, 2002, for this system.

Assuming $200,000.00 under management, the portfolio would have enjoyed an 8.48 percent average annualized return on investment over the 10-year backtested period while enduring a 19.98 percent maximum drawdown. Although these results are somewhat encouraging, traders employing this system must be willing to endure 61.18 percent losing trades, 10 consecutive losses, and lengthy intervals (almost two years) prior to achievement of new equity peaks.

It is interesting to notice how the low correlations of assets within our portfolio improved overall performance of this system. Diversification is probably among the most underemphasized benefits of system trading. A brief glance through the "totals" column shows that the portfolio's worst drawdown was only around 16 percent greater than the worst component-based drawdown. Moreover, because the portfolio's total net profits were additive and the worst drawdown was not, the profit to maximum drawdown ratio enjoyed a significant improvement when compared to almost every asset within our portfolio.

TABLE 3.2 Two moving average crossover.

Asset	Profit	# Trades	# Days	Max Draw	MDD	MCL	P:MD	P:L Ratio	%W	Time %
ES	6023	117	22	−24621	1122	7	0.24	1.07	35.90	100
TY	10678	94	27	−10681	1032	5	1.00	1.18	37.23	100
ED	5952	88	28	−5606	1577	9	1.06	1.41	32.95	100
SF	15650	121	22	−30350	565	7	0.52	1.14	40.50	100
JY	66337	112	23	−33662	1076	4	1.97	1.49	43.75	100
CL	27940	90	29	−16150	566	5	1.73	1.45	42.22	100
GC	−13600	113	23	−23210	2207	7	−0.59	0.73	36.28	100
S	−1162	103	25	−15612	1596	8	−0.07	0.98	38.83	100
LH	43490	90	29	−10210	530	7	4.26	2.03	46.67	100
CT	8155	110	23	−28870	1946	7	0.28	1.09	34.55	100
Total	**169463**	**1038**	**24.8**	**−39954**	**635**	**10**	**4.24**	**1.23**	**38.82**	**100**

Note: All trade summaries include $100 round-turn trade deductions for slippage and commissions. Data source: CQG, Inc.

ICHIMOKU TWO MOVING AVERAGE CROSSOVER

As stated in Chapter 2, the Ichimoku version of the moving average crossover has a whipsaw waiting period built in as it requires the longer-term moving average to begin turning in the direction of the crossover prior to entry.

Using CQG, the programming code for the Ichimoku two moving average crossover system is written in this way:

Long Entry and Short Exit:

```
MA(@,Sim,9)[-1] > MA(@,Sim,26)[-1]
AND MA(@,Sim,26)[-1]> MA(@,Sim,26)[-2]
```

Short Entry and Long Exit:

```
MA(@,Sim,26)[-1] < MA(@,Sim,9)[-1]
AND MA(@,Sim,26)[-1] < MA(@,Sim,26)[-2]
```

Table 3.3 presents the backtested portfolio results from December 31, 1992, to December 31, 2002, for this system.

Notice how employment of the Ichimoku's whipsaw filter led to a massive deterioration of the overall rate of return. Assuming $200,000 equity under management, our annualized rate of return drops from 8.48 percent to 1.26 percent, while the portfolio's maximum drawdown increased from 19.98 percent to 67.72 percent. If few would be willing to endure a 35 percent worse drawdown (see Chapter 8 for details), suffering through a 67.72 percent drawdown is virtually unthinkable.

TABLE 3.3 Ichimoku two moving average crossover.

Asset	Profit	# Trades	# Days	Max Draw	MDD	MCL	P:MD	P:L Ratio	%W	Time %
ES	−35907	118	22	−16694	1180	9	−0.63	0.62	23.73	100
TY	17622	103	25	−19466	1675	12	0.91	1.29	33.98	100
ED	10795	67	38	−5041	1411	9	2.14	1.96	31.34	100
SF	15325	110	24	−29062	1405	7	0.53	1.16	39.09	100
JY	27687	98	26	−62075	1934	7	0.45	1.23	45.92	100
CL	4210	124	21	−25260	1547	14	0.17	1.06	33.06	100
GC	−14380	112	23	−29520	2327	15	−0.49	0.67	29.46	100
S	−13862	99	26	−27875	2378	9	−0.50	0.76	30.03	100
LH	23230	103	25	−19700	965	9	1.18	1.46	29.13	100
CT	−9605	121	22	−49265	1916	11	−0.19	0.9	27.27	100
Total	**25115**	**1055**	**24.5**	**−153425**	**2726**	**19**	**0.16**	**1.07**	**32.13**	**100**

Note: All trade summaries include $100 round–turn trade deductions for slippage and commissions. Data source: CQG, Inc.

THREE MOVING AVERAGE CROSSOVER

As you may recall from the discussion in Chapter 2, the three moving average crossover differs from the simpler two moving average crossover in that it allows for neutrality.

Using CQG, the programming code for a typical three moving average crossover system is written in this way:

Long Entry:

```
MA(@,Sim,9)[-1] > MA(@,Sim,26)[-1] AND
MA(@,Sim,26)[-1] > MA(@,Sim,52)[-1]
```

Long Exit:

```
MA(@,Sim,9)[-1] < MA(@,Sim,26)[-1] OR MA(@,Sim,26)[-1] <
MA(@,Sim,52)[-1]
```

Short Entry:

```
MA(@,Sim,9)[-1] < MA(@,Sim,26)[-1]
AND MA(@,Sim,26)[-1] < MA(@,Sim,52)[-1]
```

Short Exit:

```
MA(@,Sim,9)[-1] > MA(@,Sim,26)[-1] OR MA(@,Sim,26)[-1] >
MA(@,Sim,52)[-1]
```

Table 3.4 presents the backtested portfolio results from December 31, 1992, to December 31, 2002, for this system.

Although the portfolio's average annualized net profit shows a vast im-

TABLE 3.4 Three moving average crossover.

Asset	Profit	# Trades	# Days	Max Draw	MDD	MCL	P:MD	P:L Ratio	%W	Time %
ES	−11605	84	21	−11530	907	9	−0.48	0.86	28.57	66.37
TY	18922	70	26	−9000	765	4	2.10	1.46	40.00	68.79
ED	6452	65	29	−5394	1523	11	1.20	1.59	33.85	73.23
SF	26462	84	22	−12875	869	5	2.06	1.40	44.05	69.43
JY	80362	76	24	−18850	411	8	4.26	2.13	50.00	68.34
CL	8730	73	23	−19840	566	8	0.44	1.18	42.47	65.59
GC	−12370	84	21	−20180	2250	7	−0.61	0.66	34.52	65.64
S	−4900	78	22	−15687	2378	9	−0.31	0.89	33.33	65.61
LH	17220	73	24	−10150	860	5	1.70	1.49	39.73	65.58
CT	9100	82	22	−21105	1946	7	0.43	1.15	35.37	67.79
Total	**138373**	**769**	**23.2**	**−51380**	**1168**	**11**	**2.69**	**1.26**	**38.1**	**67.54**

Note: All trade summaries include $100 round–turn trade deductions for slippage and commissions. Data source: CQG, Inc.

provement over the two moving average Ichimoku crossover (6.92 percent versus 1.26 percent for the two moving average Ichimoku system assuming $200,000 under management and less than 50 percent of its worst drawdown), it obviously underperformed when compared with our original two moving average crossover.

ICHIMOKU THREE MOVING AVERAGE CROSSOVER

The Ichimoku version of the three moving average crossover system not only allows for neutrality, but also has a built in whipsaw waiting period requiring both the 26- and 52-day moving averages to be trending in the direction of the crossover prior to entry.

Using CQG, the programming code for the Ichimoku three moving average crossover system is written in this way:

Long Entry:

```
MA(@,Sim,9)[-1] > MA(@,Sim,26)[-1] AND
MA(@,Sim,26)[-1] > MA(@,Sim,52)[-1] AND
MA(@,Sim,26)[-1] > MA(@,Sim,26)[-2] AND
MA(@,Sim,52)[-1] > MA(@,Sim,52)[-2]
```

Long Exit:

```
MA(@,Sim,9)[-1] < MA(@,Sim,26)[-1] OR MA(@,Sim,26)[-1] <
MA(@,Sim,52)[-1]
```

Short Entry:

```
MA(@,Sim,9)[-1] < MA(@,Sim,26)[-1] AND
MA(@,Sim,26)[-1] < MA(@,Sim,52)[-1] AND
MA(@,Sim,26)[-1] < MA(@,Sim,26)[-2] AND
MA(@,Sim,52)[-1] < MA(@,Sim,52)[-2]
```

Short Exit:

```
MA(@,Sim,9) [-1] > MA(@,Sim,26)[-1] OR MA(@,Sim,26)[-1] >
MA(@,Sim,52)[-1]
```

Table 3.5 presents the backtested portfolio results from December 31, 1992, to December 31, 2002, for this system.

Notice that the three moving average Ichimoku generated superior results to the simple three moving average crossover. This is in stark contrast to our comparison of the two moving average crossover and the two mov-

TABLE 3.5 Three moving average Ichimoku cross-over.

Asset	Profit	# Trades	# Days	Max Draw	MDD	MCL	P:MD	P:L Ratio	%W	Time %
ES	−17869	75	22	−9330	907	7	−0.57	0.75	30.67	62.44
TY	21525	56	30	−10931	556	4	1.97	1.61	42.86	64.97
ED	7471	58	32	−5106	1518	10	1.46	1.80	34.48	70.64
SF	32550	72	24	−11275	541	5	2.89	1.60	44.44	64.57
JY	81462	62	27	−16837	649	6	4.84	2.04	48.39	64.00
CL	9610	61	27	−21750	702	7	0.44	1.22	42.62	62.35
GC	−12680	73	22	−20560	2357	6	−0.62	0.65	32.88	61.45
S	−2800	64	25	−14712	2378	7	−0.19	0.93	34.37	61.80
LH	15690	63	26	−10610	1014	4	1.48	1.45	41.27	62.68
CT	18270	68	24	−16360	1946	8	1.12	1.38	36.76	62.58
Total	**153229**	**652**	**25.6**	**−50911**	**1168**	**10**	**3.01**	**1.35**	**38.65**	**63.62**

Note: All trade summaries include $100 round–turn trade deductions for slippage and commissions. Data source: CQG, Inc.

ing average Ichimoku. This reversal illustrates the problems encountered when attempting to generalize rules of performance from a single example. If, after our comparison of the regular and Ichimoku two moving average crossovers, we incorrectly concluded that Ichimoku would always underperform and eliminated it from future examination, we would have discarded the second best performing crossover system of the four analyzed.

MACD

Obviously there are various methods of generating trend-following trading systems with MACD. This section shows one of the simplest applications of a stop-and-reverse MACD trend-following system based on MACD crossing the MACD's signal line and the signal line crossing the zero level. Readers are strongly encouraged to view this rudimentary system as a prototype in developing their own strategies.

Using CQG, the programming code for a simple MACD stop and reverse trading system is written in this way:

Long Entry and Short Exit:

```
MACD(@,13.000,26.000)[-1] XABOVE MACDA(@,13.000,26.000,9.000)[-1]
AND MACDA(@,13.000,26.000,9.000)[-1] > 0
```

Short Entry and Long Exit:

```
MACD(@,13.000,26.000)[-1] XBELOW MACDA(@,13.000,26.000,9.000) [-1]
AND MACDA(@,13.000,26.000,9.000)[-1] < 0
```

TABLE 3.6   MACD.

Asset	Profit	# Trades	# Days	Max Draw	MDD	MCL	P:MD	P:L Ratio	%W	Time %
ES	−4242	19	133	−42446	1089	4	−0.10	0.91	36.84	100
TY	35678	19	132	−12875	810	5	2.77	3.10	47.37	100
ED	9097	15	165	−6812	1827	8	1.34	2.60	26.67	100
SF	58225	14	179	−20225	516	3	2.88	3.72	57.14	100
JY	37	18	137	−41500	1098	2	0.00	1.00	44.44	100
CL	61080	14	179	−19840	521	5	3.08	4.75	42.86	100
GC	740	22	113	−13810	985	6	0.05	1.04	36.36	100
S	−18812	23	110	−35325	2378	5	−0.53	0.61	34.78	100
LH	21440	18	139	−11690	688	4	1.83	1.94	50.00	100
CT	56255	13	193	−13990	510	1	4.02	6.43	61.54	100
Total	**219498**	**175**	**142.9**	**−42554**	**686**	**7**	**5.16**	**2.34**	**42.85**	**100**

Note: All trade summaries include $100 round–turn trade deductions for slippage and commissions. Data source: CQG, Inc.

Table 3.6 presents the backtested portfolio results from December 31, 1992, to December 31, 2002, for this system.

Although these results are mildly encouraging, most people do not have the patience and fortitude to sit with a trade for an average of 143 days, and doing so is an absolute prerequisite for successful implementation of this particular system. Obviously various filters could be introduced to modify this characteristic; however, it is highlighted here to illustrate considerations in trading a system beyond mere analysis of risk versus return on investment or total net profit.

DMI

This simple modification of the stop and reverse systems employed above minimizes whipsaws as the market oscillates above and below the zero level. Instead of entries triggered around the zero level, I set the long entry criteria to +20 or greater and short entry to −20 or lower. (Note: Altering trigger points away from the zero level to reduce whipsaws is also applicable to all of the trend-following conditional trading systems, including the two moving average crossovers, MACD, momentum, and ROC.)

Using CQG, the programming code for our DMI trading system is written in this way:

Long Entry:

```
DDIF(@,10)[-1] XABOVE 20
```

Long Exit:

```
DDIF(@,10[-1] XBELOW 0
```

Short Entry:

```
DDIF(@,10)[-1] XBELOW -20
```

Short Exit:

```
DDIF(@,10[-1] XABOVE 0
```

Table 3.7 presents the backtested portfolio results from December 31, 1992, to December 31, 2002, for this system.

A quick glance at the numbers shows this system's backtested portfolio results are inferior to almost all of those examined earlier. Readers are encouraged to experiment with adding filters, such as implied volatility of options on the underlying asset breaking above the upper/lower Bollinger bands as confirming entry criteria. If implied volatility were trending up, a filter might improve our probability of participating in a sustainable trending market, thereby transforming a marginally profitable system into a viable one.[5]

DMI WITH ADX

Because Wilder's original presentation of DMI was linked with ADX, next I present readers the results from the addition of this filter to our original DMI system.

TABLE 3.7 DMI.

Asset	Profit	# Trades	# Days	Max Draw	MDD	MCL	P:MD	P:L Ratio	%W	Time %
ES	−25911	87	17	−33251	1424	15	−0.78	0.62	29.89	53.99
TY	1037	84	19	−13309	2393	6	0.08	1.02	33.33	58.70
ED	3287	73	24	−4319	1878	7	0.76	1.28	34.25	67.69
SF	6700	79	19	−20412	1325	7	0.33	1.10	44.30	55.11
JY	43325	87	18	−20675	460	6	2.10	1.47	41.38	58.85
CL	22160	73	20	−8190	610	6	2.71	1.54	45.21	56.03
GC	−18170	99	15	−24600	2402	13	−0.74	0.57	26.26	55.05
S	−6962	79	18	−12487	1292	9	−0.56	0.85	31.65	52.58
LH	24230	72	22	−10640	694	8	2.28	1.77	44.44	60.06
CT	9105	74	19	−29480	1948	7	0.31	1.15	40.54	53.18
Total	**58801**	**807**	**18.9**	**−30459**	**1239**	**17**	**1.93**	**1.11**	**36.68**	**57.00**

Note: All trade summaries include $100 round–turn trade deductions for slippage and commissions. Data source: CQG, Inc.

Using CQG, the programming code for a simple DMI trading system with an ADX filter is written in this way:

Long Entry:

```
DDIF(@,10)[-1] XABOVE 20 AND ADX(@,9)[-1] > 20
```

Long Exit:

```
DDIF(@,10)[-1] XBELOW 0 OR ADX(@,9)[-1] < 20
```

Short Entry:

```
DDIF(@,10)[-1] XBELOW -20 AND ADX(@,9)[-1] > 20
```

Short Exit:

```
DDIF(@,10)[-1] XABOVE 0 OR ADX(@,9)[-1] < 20
```

Table 3.8 presents the backtested portfolio results from December 31, 1992, to December 31, 2002, for this system.

Notice that addition of the ADX filter worsened overall performance. Although one example does not prove that an indicator should be discarded (as proved by our examination of Ichimoku), it does suggest that combining of indicators simply because data vendors or indicator developers link them will not necessarily increase profitability.

TABLE 3.8   DMI with ADX filter.

Asset	Profit	# Trades	# Days	Max Draw	MDD	MCL	P:MD	P:L Ratio	%W	Time %
ES	−18652	86	16	−30243	1424	12	−0.62	0.69	31.4	52.40
TY	−1431	84	18	−18406	2466	9	−0.08	0.97	32.14	56.72
ED	1556	76	23	−4181	2056	7	0.37	1.13	30.26	66.23
SF	−2537	81	17	−21850	1324	5	−0.12	0.96	41.98	52.99
JY	41825	85	17	−18300	952	3	2.29	1.46	41.18	55.61
CL	7490	73	19	−15170	623	6	0.49	1.16	38.36	54.00
GC	−18080	97	15	−25020	2401	22	−0.72	0.57	23.71	52.90
S	−8925	80	17	−14525	2378	10	−0.61	0.80	31.25	51.63
LH	25470	73	21	−9940	689	7	2.56	1.78	46.58	59.07
CT	18195	73	19	−21280	1947	7	0.85	1.35	42.47	52.10
Total	**44911**	**808**	**18**	**−27256**	**885**	**17**	**1.65**	**1.07**	**35.52**	**55.25**

Note: All trade summaries include $100 round–turn trade deductions for slippage and commissions. Data source: CQG, Inc.

CHANNEL BREAKOUT

As stated in Chapter 2, channel breakout is a purely price-triggered trend-following system. Although our backtest will employ Donchian's original 20-day stop and reverse parameters, readers are encouraged to experiment with modifications, including lengthening the parameter (e.g., setting n period to 70) to reduce false breakouts, as well as changing the exit condition (e.g., entry when market breaks 20-day highs/lows and exit when it breaks 10-day highs/low) to transform the stop and reverse system into one that allows for neutrality.

Because the original parameters proposed by Donchian do not account for shifts in market volatility per se, another worthwhile experiment is the examination of filters that would cut loses during periods of high volatility. A simple example of this approach would be the addition of a stop loss based on 1 to 5 percent of the asset's value at the time of entry (see the "Cutting Losses" section later in this chapter).

Another potential drawback to Donchian's approach is that signals are triggered at or just beyond horizontal support and resistance levels. This could potentially entice large speculative players to trigger stops positioned at these levels, resulting in false breakouts. Readers are encouraged to experiment with various solutions to the problem. One particularly simple and robust solution is offered by Art Collins, author of numerous articles on trading systems, who proposes the addition of a filter requiring the market to break the n period level by 20 percent of the prior trading day's range.[6]

If you examine the programming code below closely, you will notice that I have made one very minor modification to the traditional channel breakout system: entry and exits at the prior 20-day high or low instead of the traditional greater than or less than 20-day high or low. Since many countertrend traders fade old resistance and support levels, this minor adjustment gives me greater confidence that our $100 slippage/commissions deduction will remain a realistic assumption.

Using CQG, the programming code for the 20-day stop and reverse channel breakout system is written in this way:

For Long Entry and Short Exit, set "Price" field to:

```
HiLevel(@,20)[-1]
```

For Short Entry and Long Exit, set "Price" field to:

```
LoLevel(@,20)[-1]
```

Table 3.9 presents the backtested portfolio results from December 31, 1992, to December 31, 2002, for this system.

TABLE 3.9 Channel breakout.

Asset	Profit	# Trades	# Days	Max Draw	MDD	MCL	P:MD	P:L Ratio	%W	Time %
ES	11269	75	35	−27001	798	7	0.42	1.19	34.67	100
TY	28437	65	40	−15300	1252	5	1.86	1.67	43.08	100
ED	−4125	85	31	−10080	1903	9	−0.41	0.83	25.88	100
SF	27812	68	38	−17625	561	5	1.58	1.33	45.59	100
JY	63475	74	35	−20125	994	4	3.15	1.59	39.19	100
CL	8130	76	34	−23190	743	6	0.35	1.12	42.11	100
GC	−780	78	33	−9490	2250	7	−0.08	0.98	30.77	100
S	5337	78	33	−16375	1760	4	0.33	1.10	37.18	100
LH	36400	73	36	−10630	664	5	3.42	1.94	52.05	100
CT	−16920	87	30	−38060	1947	7	−0.44	0.83	28.74	100
Total	**159035**	**759**	**34.3**	**−44898**	**749**	**19**	**3.54**	**1.24**	**37.42**	**100**

Note: All trade summaries include $100 round–turn trade deductions for slippage and commissions. Data source: CQG, Inc.

BOLLINGER BANDS

Here I offer a simple trend-following breakout system where entry signals are triggered by the market closing beyond the upper or lower bands. The system exits open positions when markets revert to the mean (e.g., the 20-day simple moving average). Using CQG, the programming code for this Bollinger band breakout system is written in this way:

Long Entry:

```
Close(@)[-1] > BHI(@,Sim,20,2.00)[-1]
```

Short Entry:

```
Close(@)[-1] < BLO(@,Sim,20,2.00)[-1]
```

Long Exit and Short Exit set "Price" field to:

```
BMA(@,Sim,20)[-1]
```

Table 3.10 presents the backtested portfolio results from December 31, 1992, to December 31, 2002, for this system.

Notice that although this system suffered through 17 consecutive losses, the low correlation of assets within the portfolio still resulted in the endurance of a less severe worst drawdown than that experienced by trading the E-mini S&P 500 by itself.

SOME COMPARISONS

Bollinger Band System and the Three Moving Average Ichimoku

Although a glance at the total net profit column might suggest the three moving average Ichimoku crossover (Table 3.5) was the superior performer, this conclusion is incorrect. While it is true that our Bollinger band system (Table 3.10) produced only a total net profit of $107,396 versus $153,229 for the three moving average Ichimoku, this does not tell the whole story.

Assuming $200,000 equity under management, the three moving average Ichimoku enjoyed an average annualized return on investment of 7.66 percent with a 25.46 percent worst drawdown. By contrast, based on the same assumptions, the Bollinger Band system would have experienced a similar 5.37 percent average annualized rate of return while enduring almost 50 percent less risk (its maximum drawdown was 14.16 percent). In other words, if we examine total net profit in relation to the risks endured to achieve those profits, Bollinger Bands were the better performer. This is illustrated by its superior profit to maximum drawdown (P:MD) ratio of 3.79 percent versus 3.01 percent for the three moving average Ichimoku.

This comparison shows the importance of not analyzing total net profit in a vacuum. By itself, this measure is meaningless. It must always be viewed in relation to maximum drawdown to gauge reward in relation to risk. Moreover, although its results were inferior to the three moving average crossover in terms of total net profit, the Bollinger bands system achieved its superior P:MD while tying up investment capital less often.

TABLE 3.10 Bollinger bands.

Asset	Profit	# Trades	# Days	Max Draw	MDD	MCL	P:MD	P:L Ratio	%W	Time %
ES	−20113	97	13	−39957	1358	9	−0.50	0.71	36.08	44.72
TY	6195	97	15	−12296	2088	11	0.50	1.14	39.18	52.07
ED	1704	83	17	−6066	1783	10	0.28	1.15	33.73	53.40
SF	25486	91	15	−16374	1058	8	1.56	1.43	36.26	51.09
JY	67096	79	19	−11773	388	3	5.70	1.90	48.1	56.26
CL	7305	97	15	−12815	528	7	0.57	1.13	34.02	54.21
GC	−13157	96	15	−19969	2327	9	−0.66	0.65	29.17	50.32
S	−31	91	13	14914	1461	8	0.00	1.00	34.07	44.70
LH	14615	88	18	−16181	770	6	0.90	1.36	43.18	54.88
CT	18296	100	14	−24762	1947	9	0.74	1.31	34.00	51.36
Total	**107396**	**919**	**15.3**	**−28323**	**727**	**17**	**3.79**	**1.16**	**36.56**	**51.18**

Note: All trade summaries include $100 round–turn trade deductions for slippage and commissions. Data source: CQG, Inc.

MACD versus Bollinger Bands

In this comparison MACD is obviously the superior performing system. Not only does it enjoy a better P:MD, but it does so while enjoying a higher percentage of winning trades, better profit-to-loss ratio, and fewer consecutive losses. So why would anyone choose to trade the Bollinger bands system?

The most obvious reason is that MACD's results were achievable only if one had the prerequisite $200,000 in equity under management needed to withstand its maximum drawdown. If one had only $100,000 under management, employment of MACD would entail the weathering of a 42.55 percent maximum drawdown (compared to a 28.32% drawdown for the Bollinger band system). Moreover, remember that MACD's superior performance was only achievable if one had the patience and fortitude to hold trades for an average of 143 days.

If a trader showed me the results from Tables 3.10 (Bollinger bands) and 3.6 (MACD), then asked which I thought was the better trading strategy, I would pose four questions:

1. How much equity is available to trade this strategy?
2. Are you more comfortable holding a trade an average of 15 or 143 days?
3. Is it easier for you to hold fewer trades and always have a position in the market or to trade with greater frequency and be out of the market around 49 percent of the time?
4. Do you possess the discipline and fortitude required to stick with a trading system that will endure 17 consecutive losses, or is withstanding 7 a more realistic accomplishment?

Obviously there is no single right or wrong answer to these questions; it all depends on an individual trader's temperament. Although the answers to these questions are of far greater importance than theoretical backtested returns on investment, most traders will continue dedicating investment capital to a system based on its theoretical returns irrespective of their psychological compatibility with that system.

The point is, unless someone's personality is well suited to trading a particular system over the next 10 to 30 years, "theoretical" returns are destined to remain just that: theoretical. The implementation of an incompatible system will raise all the same psychological issues as trying to trade without a system—a breakdown in discipline, lack of patience, and an inability to withstand drawdowns in equity, consecutive losses, and low winning percentages.

GENERAL RULES OF THUMB

Filters

Although I encourage readers to experiment with the addition of various filters to the simple trend-following systems just outlined, I believe that the more conditions added, the lower the probability of replication of similar results in the future. Even though the backtested results just shown entail large peak-to-valley equity drawdowns, low percentage of winning trades, and mediocre rate of return, I prefer knowing that my backtested drawdowns have less likelihood of being exceeded in the future. This gives me greater confidence during the weathering of real time equity drawdowns. This psychological confidence during drawdowns factor should not be underestimated, because it is our ability to stick with the trend-following system during a string of consecutive losses that will determine our success as trend-following system traders.

As opposed to optimizing the results of simple trend-following systems through the addition of multiple filters, I prefer to accept a low percentage of winning trades and large consecutive string of losing trades, and instead focus my efforts on development and disciplined adherence to stringent price risk management techniques that are robust enough to weather all equity drawdowns except those that entail a questioning of the system's continued viability.

Trending Asset Classes

In reviewing portfolio results of these trend-following systems, time and again we see that specific asset classes produced the lion's share of the trend-following system's profits. This raises several questions. The most obvious is: Why do asset classes like foreign currencies and short-term interest rates generate so much of our overall profits? Although I am not a fundamental analyst, I would argue that these markets tend to exhibit more consistent "trending" behavior because central banks have greater influence over their direction via short-term interest rate policies than in markets such as equity indices.

The next glaring observation is that equity indices perform poorly in trend-following systems (see Table 3.11). Here again my feeling is that these intermediate-term trend-following systems fall victim to the whipsaw nature of these assets. I believe equity indices tend to exhibit intermediate-term choppiness as a function of the dynamic among three separate groups of participants: large short-term speculators, institutional momentum followers, and smaller, undercapitalized momentum followers. Typically the

TABLE 3.11 Asset classes: historical tendencies.

Trending[a]	Mid	Mean Reverting
Currencies vs. dollar	Most physical commodities	Equity Indices
Short-term interest rates	Mid- and long-term rates	Most FX crosses[b]

[a]These are historical tendencies that I have noticed as of this writing. The character and dynamics of various asset classes can and will change over time; therefore, continuous monitoring of these tendencies is essential.

[b]Foreign exchange crosses are defined as non–U.S. dollar–denominated cross rates, such are euro-yen; British pound-Swiss franc.

Data source: CQG, Inc.

interplay among these groups is one in which the large short-term speculators and institutional players push the market to new highs or lows. At this point smaller, undercapitalized momentum followers initiate new positions into these market extremes as large short-term speculators take profits and fade the breakout. This, in turn, leads to capitulation of small speculators and weaker institutional momentum followers. Such capitulation usually results in quick, sharp retracements following breakouts prior to the dominant trend's reassertion.

Why do foreign exchange cross rates display a greater propensity toward mean reversion than other asset classes? My feeling is that because all currencies tend to trend against the U.S. dollar (for reasons stated earlier), as of this writing, they have exhibited a pronounced tendency toward mean reversion in relation to each other.

If certain asset classes exhibit these tendencies, why include choppy assets in trend-following system results? The simple answer is that the inclusion of assets like the S&P 500 Index ensures the robustness of our system. When our trending asset class enters a historically unprecedented and prolonged period of choppiness (e.g., IMM Japanese yen futures in 2003; for further information on this, compare Table 3.2 on page 51, earlier in this chapter, and Table 7.23 on page 153, later, in Chapter 7), we need to be confident that our price risk management tools are robust enough to ensure our survival. Inclusion of equity indices in our backtested results lets us stress test our system prior to the weathering of such an event. Obviously inclusion of mean reversion assets such as stock index futures in our backtested results has nothing to do with the composition of our real-time trend trading portfolio. In fact, I do not include such assets in a real-time portfolio, since my goal in live trading is maximizing the rate of return and minimizing risk.

CUTTING THE TAILS OF A SYSTEM'S DISTRIBUTION

Cutting Losses

One potential drawback to all indicator-driven trend-following systems is that losses tend to fluctuate on a daily basis and can be quite large if realized immediately following entry. An obvious solution to this problem is the introduction of the same type of loss limits (e.g., percentage of asset's value at entry) examined in our discussion of channel breakout filters. I strongly encourage readers to experiment with various methods of cutting off the left (or loss) tail of their trend-following system's distribution, especially if the system is intermediate to long term and per-trade losses suffered would otherwise be large in relation to average per-trade profits.

Figure 3.3 shows the backtested results from a simple stop-and-reverse 20-day channel breakout system; Figure 3.4 shows the same system with a stop-loss filter of 3 percent of asset value at entry.[7]

Although at first glance the simple stop and reverse channel breakout appears superior since it generated a larger total net profit, notice that the

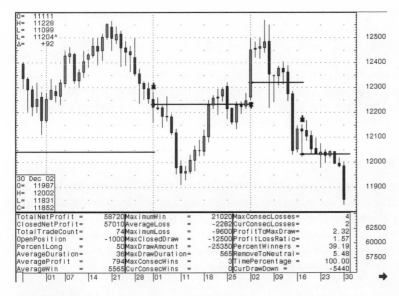

O=	11111
H=	11228
L=	11099
L=	11204^
Δ=	+92

30 Dec 02	
O=	11987
H=	12002
L=	11831
C=	11852

TotalNetProfit =	58720	MaximumWin =	21020	MaxConsecLosses=	4
ClosedNetProfit=	57010	AverageLoss =	-2282	CurConsecLosses=	2
TotalTradeCount=	74	MaximumLoss =	-9600	ProfitToMaxDraw=	2.32
OpenPosition =	-1000	MaxClosedDraw =	-12500	ProfitLossRatio=	1.57
PercentLong =	50	MaxDrawAmount =	-25350	PercentWinners =	39.19
AverageDuration=	36	MaxDrawDuration=	565	TimePercentage =	100.00
AverageProfit =	794	MaxConsecWins =	3	RemoveToNeutral =	5.48
AverageWin =	5565	CurConsecWins =	0	CurDrawDown =	-5440

FIGURE 3.3 Spot U.S. dollar/yen with 20-day channel breakout. Includes data from December 31, 1992, to December 31, 2002.

Note: All trade summaries include $100 round-turn trade deductions for slippage and commissions. ©2004 CQG, Inc. All rights reserved worldwide.

FIGURE 3.4   Spot U.S. dollar/yen 20-day channel breakout with 3% stop loss. Includes data from December 31, 1992, to December 31, 2002.

Note: All trade summaries include $100 round-turn trade deductions for slippage and commissions. ©2004 CQG, Inc. All rights reserved worldwide.

profit to maximum drawdown (P:MD) for the system with the stop loss is larger and the time percentage required to achieve this same P:MD is smaller. Therefore, the addition of the stop loss yielded a greater return vis-à-vis risk while tying up less investor capital over time.

Cutting Profits

Many system developers advocate closing out trend-following trades once the profits accumulated on any particular trade have deviated significantly beyond the historical average per-trade profit. If we could train ourselves to act as machines, devoid of destructive emotional reactions to fluctuations in account equity or missed opportunities, then I might agree with concept of cutting profits at historically optimal levels. Unfortunately, we do react to such events.

As a result, I strongly advise newcomers to mechanical trend trading against this practice despite its occasional generation of superior "theoretical" backtested results. To fully illuminate both sides of the argument, let us compare our original MACD (Table 3.6) to MACD with the addition of a profit exit set to $2,500, as shown in Table 3.12.

TABLE 3.12 MACD with profit exit of $2,500.

Asset	Profit	# Trades	# Days	Max Draw	MDD	MCL	P:MD	P:L Ratio	%W	Time %
ES	19829	41	46	−21720	912	2	0.91	1.44	68.29	72.84
TY	29812	40	46	−10747	750	3	2.77	1.90	65.00	72.61
ED	7722	19	125	−6812	1853	8	1.13	2.36	42.11	93.87
SF	40462	42	45	−20225	956	3	2.00	2.05	76.19	73.28
JY	13200	46	27	−29412	1480	2	0.45	1.16	80.43	48.07
CL	40590	38	46	−14370	520	3	2.82	2.48	73.68	68.05
GC	−1270	29	79	−13810	975	6	−0.09	0.95	41.38	90.85
S	−23937	33	63	−31425	2325	5	−0.76	0.59	45.45	81.84
LH	10460	32	52	−11170	823	3	0.94	1.29	62.50	64.61
CT	36095	35	47	−13845	359	2	2.61	2.33	77.14	65.02
Total	**172963**	**355**	**52.6**	**−40477**	**570**	**6**	**4.27**	**1.64**	**65.63**	**71.07**

Note: All trade summaries include $100 round–turn trade deductions for slippage and commissions. Data source: CQG, Inc.

Notice that despite its inferior profit to maximum drawdown (P:MD), the addition the $2,500 profit exit did improve many aspects of our original MACD system: a superior win/loss ratio, reduction of maximum drawdown duration, and average trade duration along with a lower percentage of time that our capital was employed in the markets.

Some system developers might contend that this comparison is unrealistic because it only cuts off profitable outliers, whereas most traders would cut off both the profit and the loss tails of the distribution. Table 3.13 shows the performance results of the MACD system with the addition of both a profit exit and a stop loss set to $2,500.

Clearly this version of the system is inferior to the others. The equalization of profits and losses in a trending environment would produce superior results only if markets trended more often than they reverted to the mean.

Even if our comparisons had shown the achievement of superior performance through the cutting of profits, I would still have strongly advised against the practice. My contention is that the main purpose in adopting mechanical trading systems is reinforcement of positive trader psychology and elimination of destructive behavioral habits. Furthermore, although the theory of generating a smoother distribution of returns by elimination of outliers may sound appealing to statisticians and system developers, the reality of taking what appears to be an optimal profit off the table only to witness its doubling or tripling is absolutely devastating to trader morale and discipline.

With the exception of huge losses, nothing leads to the psychological derailment of inexperienced trend traders' discipline than watching the

TABLE 3.13 MACD with profit and stop exit of $2,500.

Asset	Profit	# Trades	# Days	Max Draw	MDD	MCL	P:MD	P:L Ratio	%W	Time %
ES	−5753	48	29	−21530	1356	4	−0.27	0.90	47.92	53.95
TY	15262	43	37	−11728	975	5	1.30	1.37	53.49	61.39
ED	7697	19	125	−6812	1853	8	1.13	2.36	42.11	93.87
SF	12400	52	19	−9925	987	3	1.25	1.21	55.77	36.89
JY	19512	53	12	−14512	1374	5	1.34	1.33	58.49	23.01
CL	28810	40	33	−15320	564	6	1.88	1.90	62.50	51.44
GC	−9230	33	63	−19750	1239	6	−0.47	0.72	36.36	81.17
S	−13537	38	38	−16800	2324	6	−0.81	0.72	39.47	55.92
LH	3220	32	41	−8230	754	3	0.39	1.09	53.12	50.77
CT	31995	38	29	−7725	373	3	4.14	2.13	68.42	42.48
Total	**90376**	**396**	**36**	**−30000**	**1064**	**8**	**3.01**	**1.32**	**52.78**	**52.44**

Note: All trade summaries include $100 round-turn trade deductions for slippage and commissions. Data source: CQG, Inc.

massive accumulation of would-be profits from the sidelines as they are forced to settle for safely banked, so-called optimal rates of return. Although elimination of historical outliers sounds like the prudent, scientific path, in practice it is emotionally crippling. Traders who advocate elimination of the outliers usually are unwilling to let profits run and have an irrational desire to control the markets, particularly to control the level of their per-trade profits.

I call this process of inexperienced trend traders losing their position and/or missing a profitable trade the sideline regret/remorse syndrome. When it manifests as the relinquishing of a winning position, the decision to bank profits usually stems from a fear of those significant profits turning into small profits. As the market continues trending, traders feel regret and remorse, which can be alleviated only through the loss of discipline or participating in the trend irrespective of price risk management considerations. Often this throwing-in-the-towel mentality is pure crowd following and results in entry at the blowoff phase of the trend. Because reentry was triggered by emotion irrespective of risk, these traders tend to hold onto the losing trade until it balloons to the capitulation point. Then this failure can lead either to self-chastisement, lack of confidence, and trader paralysis (the inability to initiate new trades) or to a reckless gambler mentality that I call the breakeven syndrome.

The breakeven syndrome is one in which traders rationalize away prudent rules of price risk management as a temporary abandonment that they will return to once they break even. What I will say from years of experience is that once discipline is broken, only pain and failure will motivate us to resuscitate it.

Why does this loss of discipline/premature relinquishing of positions occur? Usually newcomers' temptation to eliminate the outliers grows stronger after a large unrealized profit gives back a significant portion of potential gains. We can put these situations into perspective by remembering two things:

1. No one ever captures the top or bottom of a trend, and only with hindsight is a particular exit point apparent.

2. As trend traders, because a small percentage of all trend-following trades will make up a large portion of our profits, cutting off the outliers hampers our ability to financially weather the equity drawdowns that are inherent in any trend-following strategy and increases our risk of ruin.

If readers still are tempted by superior theoretical performance promised through cutting profits and are disciplined enough to adhere to the system irrespective of short-term pain/regret, I urge you to employ some mechanized methodology that forces you back into formerly abandoned trend trades once it is apparent that the dominant trend has asserted itself again.

PSYCHOLOGICAL PROFILE OF A TREND-FOLLOWING TRADER

Although this profile is by no means exhaustive, I believe it will give readers enough of an understanding of the trend trader's personality traits to accurately assess their ability to implement these strategies successfully.

- *Willingness to buy recent highs/sell recent lows.* Unless traders adhere to this first premise, there is no point in reading on. Trend trading works because it is extremely difficult to buy highs and sell lows.
  Psychological reminders to help with this problem:
  - If trend trading were easy, then everyone could do it and it would not be a profitable strategy.
  - When feelings of uneasiness, fear, and apprehension arise in anticipation of buying recent highs (selling recent lows), reprogram yourself to associate these feelings with success and profitability. (Reinforce this reprogramming with a review of the backtested results shown in this chapter.)
- *Willingness to give back a significant portion of unrealized gains.* Remember that no one knows when the trend will end. Instead of attempting to anticipate the trend's reversal, sit back and allow profits to accumulate.

As we have been programmed to associate being right with success and being wrong with failure, it is only natural for us to remember and focus on those instances in which our intuition told us that we were at the top or bottom (therefore, not forced to relinquish a portion of profits) and conveniently forget times when our predicted market turns did not come to fruition. I call this phenomenon the psychic trader syndrome.

Psychological reminders to help with this problem:

○ Participate, don't anticipate.
○ The market pays us handsomely for our patience. Regret over giving back a portion of one's profits is only obvious with hindsight.
○ Keeping a daily trading journal of your market forecasts will aid in abandonment of the psychic trader syndrome.

- *Willingness to exhibit patience through numerous, consecutive small losses.* Patience is the key to success as a trend trader. Psychological reminder to help with this problem:

○ Backtesting and analysis of a mechanical trading system's results will help in recognizing that sticking to the strategy after consecutive losses eventually leads to profitability. This historical trade evaluation process fosters the courage, fortitude, and discipline needed to weather such losses.

- *Ability to blend discipline with flexibility.* Discipline suggests sticking to the successful strategy; flexibility suggests abandonment of a strategy once markets have undergone a paradigm shift.[8]

Although discipline and flexibility appear to be mutually exclusive concepts, the most successful traders believe in their strategies and are willing to stick with them through tough periods. Simultaneously, they are always cognizant of the ever-shifting nature of the markets and open to adapting or even abandoning their strategies when market behavior undergoes paradigms shifts.

- *Willingness to trade small enough (e.g., not risking over 1 to 5 percent of equity under management on any single position) to withstand the drawdowns entailed when employing a trend-following strategy.* This problem can stem from two opposite experiences: the breakeven syndrome, where we overleverage ourselves to bounce back from losses more quickly, and a form of the regret/remorse syndrome, where we look at booked profits and decide to increase leverage to capture larger rates of returns.

Psychological reminder to help with this problem:

○ Look at the percentage of winning trades in the backtested history along with the worst peak to valley drawdowns in equity. Then remember, if you do not trade small enough to withstand an unprecedented drawdown, you will not be around long enough to become profitable.

- *Ability to be comfortable with 1 to 5 percent of trades executed generating most profits.* This realization is closely linked with one of the primary rules of mechanical trend trading: Never miss a trading signal. This means no vacations from trading ever. Eliminate the top performers from your backtested history (see Table 3.12) and you will quickly recognize that vacations and mechanical trend trading do not mix. Also, since 1 to 5 percent of trades will generate the majority of profits, trading systems must include a reentry mechanism if the trend reasserts itself.

  Psychological reminder to help with this problem:
  - Examine your system's historical performance excluding these top-performing trades.

- *Willingness to stay with open positions for weeks to months.* Trend traders succeed because they know how to let small profits grow large. This entails a willingness to stay with open positions for weeks or even months.

  Psychological tools to help with this issue:
  - Stay away from the computer screen during trading hours (especially during the early stages of your career as a trend trader).
  - Trade around the core position—this helps with the psychological problem of thinking you need to earn your pay by being active while not sacrificing your position. By adding a second contract and/or trading around the core position, you guarantee participation in the trend and can satisfy the psychological need to be active. Of course, the caveat to trading around the core position is that the addition of this second contract should not result in large percentage drawdowns.

- *Ability to be comfortable with slower, more analytical trading processes.* Many trend trader personality types feel overwhelmed at the prospect of making numerous decisions throughout the trading day. Psychological reminder to help with this problem:
  - People with this personality type find holding intermediate or long-term positions less stressful, especially since they can walk away from the screen throughout the trading day.

CHAPTER 4

Mean Reversion Systems

A Matter of Patience

Buy when the cannons are firing and sell when the trumpets sound victory.

—Baron Rothschild

CONSIDERATIONS IN ANALYZING INTERMEDIATE-TERM MEAN REVERSION TRADING SYSTEMS

Because markets are range-bound more often than they trend, mean reversion systems tend to enjoy a higher percentage of winning trades than trend-following systems. But because our goal in trading a mean reversion system is entering at temporarily unsustainable levels and exiting at the average, our profit to loss ratios and overall performance often will be inferior to that experienced with successful trend-following systems.

This does not suggest that mean reversion traders are less successful than trend traders; instead, it clues us in to the fact that top-caliber mean reversion traders usually augment basic mechanical trading techniques with discretionary elements. In other words, mean reversion traders may need to incorporate elements that cannot easily be quantified into a mechanical trading, such as unsustainable emotionalism, government reports, wars, and natural disasters.

Achievement of Profit Target and Stop Loss on Same Day

When analyzing backtested results of intermediate-term mean reversion systems, there is a higher probability of the market reaching both the stop loss and profit level on the same trading day. Ideally an analysis of intraday data would show whether the trade was a profit or loss, but as of this writing, no data vendors offer 10 to 20 years' worth of intraday price history. As a result, in such instances I will assume that these trades were stopped out as losses.

Stop Losses

In real-time trading the use of stops based on percentage of contract value at time of entry is a sound methodology. Unfortunately, because futures contracts are included in our backtested portfolio and valuation of these assets is based on a continuously adjusted data series, these assets could have a hypothetical value of zero, and percentage-based stops would distort our backtested results.

    The use of a fixed dollar amount stop loss is also an imperfect solution. Because the asset's value over the length of the backtested period will vary significantly, using fixed dollar stops could underestimate or overestimate the true risk inherent in these trades (as demonstrated in Chapter 3's percentage value comparison of natural gas when futures prices rose from $1.50 to $6.00). Despite this potential distortion, I employ a fixed dollar stop level in one of the backtested portfolio results (see relative strength index extremes with 200-day moving average filter, page 77).

    If the components within a portfolio are prone to significant distortions due to changes in asset valuation throughout the backtested period, I suggest employment of some indicator-driven stop loss, such as placement of stops 2.5 standard deviations beyond the 20-day moving average. (This is just one of many robust solutions to the backtested data problems. Readers are encouraged to experiment with other stop-level methodologies.)

TREND-FOLLOWING MEAN REVERSION SYSTEMS

Some trading systems can easily be tailored to capitalize on reversion to the mean while still trading in the direction of the long-term trend. Although they are not without drawbacks, these systems are often easier for new traders to stick with—assuming they have already mastered the discipline required to fade mass psychology—because they enter at recent market extremes (selling recent highs or buying recent lows), while simultaneously trading in the direction of the longer-term trend (which results in greater confidence during drawdowns).

    In addition, because these are mean reversion systems, traders exit with profits once the market reverts back to the average. Because both risk and reward are quantified at the time of the trade's initiation, one of the most difficult psychological obstacles to successful trend trading—letting profits run—has been eliminated.

Relative Strength Index Extremes with 200-Day Moving Average Filter

This system waits for the market to achieve extreme overbought or oversold relative strength index (RSI) levels while still trading in the direction of the long-term trend through its use of a 200-day moving average as a filter. Because we are trading the direction of the long-term trend, we can place our exit with profit criteria levels somewhere beyond the mean. In this case we exit long positions when the 14-day RSI crosses beyond the 60 level and exit shorts when the 40 level is breached.

As discussed in Chapter 2, we will need to include a second, fail-safe exit condition to protect us against unlimited loss in the event that the trend changes and the market does not revert to its mean.

Using CQG, the programming code for the trend-following mean reversion system with RSI extremes, 200-day moving average filter, and 2.5 percent stop loss is written as:

Long Entry:

```
RSI(@,9)[-1] < 35 AND Close(@)[-1] > MA(@,Sim,200)[-1]
```

Long Exit—Condition #1:

```
RSI(@,14)[-1] XABOVE 60
```

Long Exit—Condition #2:

```
EntryPrice(@,0,All,ThisTradeOnly)-(.025*
EntryPrice(@,0,All,ThisTradeOnly))
```

Short Entry:

```
RSI(@,9)[-1] > 65 AND Close(@)[-1] < MA(@,Sim,200)[-1]
```

Short Exit—Condition #1:

```
RSI(@,14)[-1] XBELOW 40
```

Short Exit—Condition #2 set "Price" field to:

```
EntryPrice(@,0,All,ThisTradeOnly)+(.025* EntryPrice(@,0,All,
ThisTradeOnly))
```

The programming code just shown is fine for backtesting of cash contracts. However, if we want to backtest this system on our futures portfolio, we cannot use stop losses based on percentage of contract value. Instead we will employ fixed dollar amount stop losses. Here is the long and short exit programming code for a fixed $2,500 stop loss:

Set "Price" field to:

```
OpenPositionAverageEntryPrice(@,ThisTradeOnly) -
Dollar2Price(@,2500) / OpenPositionSize(@,ThisTradeOnly)
```

Due to the lack of volatility of certain assets within the portfolio, use of the $2,500 is not always realistic. Table 4.1 shows the various fixed dollar amount stops used to trade the futures portfolio.

Table 4.2 presents the results on our backtested portfolio.

Notice that the results are quite unimpressive when compared to the systems shown throughout Chapter 3. One reason for this inferior performance is that our portfolio includes eurodollars, which are not volatile enough to be profitable (especially since we have deducted $100 in slippage and commissions on a per-trade basis). How could eurodollars be volatile enough to work for our trend-following systems and not for mean reversion systems? In Chapter 3 we allowed profits to run; here we are cutting profits somewhere around the mean. Since eurodollars do not display exceptional volatility, cutting winning trades at the mean usually produces negligible per-trade profits. Subsequently, when the trend changes and the market triggers its fail-safe stop loss, such losses are substantial when compared with the small profits attained through mean reversion, resulting in an overall negative return on investment.

TABLE 4.1 Fixed dollar stops.

Asset	Stop
ES	$2,500
TY	$2,500
ED	$500
SF	$2,500
JY	$2,500
CL	$2,500
GC	$1,000
S	$1,500
LH	$1,500
CT	$2,500

TABLE 4.2 RSI extremes with 200–day moving average filter.

Asset	Profit	# Trades	# Days	Max Draw	MDD	MCL	P:MD	P:L Ratio	%W	Time %
ES	10441	39	22	–14934	1111	3	0.70	1.34	66.67	32.35
TY	–2494	34	27	–12175	2300	6	–0.20	0.90	58.82	34.83
ED	–2130	38	22	–4349	2421	5	–0.49	0.71	55.26	32.26
SF	10350	38	20	–8662	519	3	1.19	1.26	60.53	28.78
JY	–10575	43	20	–26362	1063	4	–0.40	0.85	46.51	30.87
CL	14700	43	22	–9520	1224	3	1.54	1.44	65.12	35.41
GC	2540	42	22	–7340	1546	3	0.35	1.12	64.29	34.16
S	–7325	34	25	–16512	1394	4	–0.44	0.71	50.00	32.80
LH	2950	44	21	–8500	1124	3	0.35	1.11	61.36	34.26
CT	3860	33	24	–14460	780	5	0.27	1.10	57.58	30.80
Total	**22317**	**388**	**23.4**	**–31448**	**1583**[a]	**6**	**0.71**	**1.06**	**58.76**	**32.7**

[a]Portfolio still undergoing longest drawdown at backtesting end date.
Note: All trade summaries include $100 round-turn trade deductions for slippage and commissions. Data source: CQG, Inc.

If certain assets are appropriate for backtesting of trend-following systems and not for mean reversion systems, what types of assets should be included in our mean reversion portfolio? Obviously these assets would need to exhibit greater volatility than eurodollars; beyond this volatility criterion, we would ideally like to choose assets that display a greater propensity for mean reversion than the assets chosen in Table 4.2.

Close examination of the mean reversion charts in Chapter 2 reveals that I used either the equity indices or non–U.S. dollar-denominated interbank foreign exchange cross rates exclusively. As explained in Chapter 3, historically these assets have exhibited a greater propensity toward mean reversion than other asset classes. Consequently, for the remainder of this chapter I will use the portfolio of asset shown in Table 4.3.

There are many issues to address regarding the composition of our new portfolio. The first is a review of the liquidity problem. Although foreign exchange is the most liquid of all asset classes, the majority of foreign exchange transactions are dollar denominated. Because our mean reversion portfolio will focus exclusively on non–dollar-denominated cross rates, I have decided to include only currencies of the largest, developed nations: euro, Japanese yen, British pound, Swiss franc, Canadian dollar, and Australian dollar.

A more obvious problem with the portfolio is its large weighting of foreign exchange cross rates. This could result in a high correlation of portfolio assets. In an attempt to minimize the strong positive correlation among assets within the portfolio, since the highest correlations among foreign

TABLE 4.3 Mean reversion portfolio.

Asset	Symbol	Contract Size
E-Mini S&P 500	ES	50
DM-Euro/U.S. Dollar	IEURUSD	100,000
DM-Euro/Japanese Yen	IEURJPY	1,000
DM-Euro/Swiss Franc	IEURCHF	100,000
DM-Euro/Canada $	IEURCAD	100,000
Australian $/Canada $	IAUDCAD	100,000
Canada $/Japanese Yen	ICADJPY	1,000
British Pound/Australian $	IGBPAUD	60,000
British Pound/Swiss Franc	IGBPCHF	60,000

Note: All trade summaries include $100 round-turn trade deductions for slippage and commissions. Data source: CQG, Inc.

currencies have been between the euro and Swiss franc, despite their superior performance, I have decided to eliminate cross rates such as Swiss franc–Japanese yen and Canada dollar–Swiss franc from our portfolio.

Unfortunately, the mean reversion portfolio does not have the same number of assets as its trend-following counterpart. As a result, comparisons between the two portfolios will necessarily be flawed. Although I recognize this limitation, I chose to focus on a portfolio with superior liquidity and a relatively low correlation between assets instead of the "best fit" for comparative analysis.

Finally, in Chapter 3 I chose to include one mean reverting asset in the trend-following portfolio to ensure the robustness of the trading system. Following this same reasoning, one trending asset (IEURUSD) has been included in our mean reversion portfolio.

Table 4.4 presents the backtested results from December 31, 1992, to December 31, 2002, for the RSI extremes system on our mean reversion portfolio.

As expected, performance has improved considerably when compared to Table 4.2. Nevertheless, when measured against the performance of the more robust trend-following systems examined in Chapter 3, the RSI extremes system still falls short. For example, our mean reverting system experienced a profit to maximum drawdown (P:MD) of 2.27 percent; by contrast, the two moving average system yielded a P:MD of 4.24 percent (see Table 3.2). These numbers should not surprise us; the cutting short of profits at the mean commonly results in the underperformance of mean reversion systems.

This comparison does not suggest that traders should abandon mean reversion strategies in favor of trend-following systems. It all depends on the individual trader's psychological makeup. Do not underestimate the

TABLE 4.4 RSI extremes with 200–day moving average filter and 2.5% stop.

Asset	Profit	# Trades	# Days	Max Draw	MDD	MCL	P:MD	P:L Ratio	%W	Time %
ES	8711	50	16	−14562	742	5	0.60	1.24	48.00	28.94
IEURUSD	4764	39	20	−13922	1764	6	0.34	1.10	51.28	28.99
IEURJPY	30742	46	16	−15793	557	4	1.95	1.50	58.70	27.24
IEURCHF	14902	37	28	−8343	890	2	1.79	1.65	72.97	38.63
IEURCAD	17073	42	19	−30085	1385	6	0.57	1.19	47.62	29.13
IAUDCAD	17364	33	21	−10294	937	3	1.69	1.63	66.67	25.97
ICADJPY	5681	46	20	−20425	1017	8	0.28	1.11	50.00	32.78
IGBPAUD	−9101	46	20	−24959	2541	5	−0.36	0.90	43.48	34.23
IGBPCHF	10052	33	28	−20123	791	5	0.50	1.23	60.61	34.23
Totals	**100188**	**372**	**20.4**	**−44202**	**801**	**11**	**2.27**	**1.27**	**54.57**	**31.06**

Note: All trade summaries include $100 round-turn trade deductions for slippage and commissions. Data source: CQG, Inc.

value of superior results in columns such as percentage of winning trades and maximum consecutive losses. (Note: Although this particular system experienced a large string of consecutive losses, as will be shown in Tables 4.5 and 4.6, this is usually not the case.) Experiencing more winning trades than losing ones or enduring a smaller string of consecutive losses can make the difference between sticking with a particular trading system long enough to reap its rewards and abandoning it.

Bollinger Bands with 200-day Moving Average Filter

One of the pitfalls of RSI extremes was that the average duration of a trade was the same as that of our intermediate-term trend-following systems. This problem can be eliminated by changing its exit condition #1 criteria, but to showcase another trend-following mean reversion system, I have chosen instead to introduce the fading of our trend-following Bollinger band system with the addition of a 200-day moving average criteria to filter out countertrend trades.

Using CQG, the programming code for this trend-following mean reversion system is written in this way:

Long Entry:

```
Close(@)[-1] XBELOW BLO(@,Sim,20,2)[-1]AND
Close(@)[-1] > MA(@,Sim,200)[-1]
```

Long Exit—Condition #1 set "Price" field to:

```
BMA(@,Sim,20)[-1]
```

Long Exit—Condition #2 set "Price" field to:

```
EntryPrice(@,0,All,ThisTradeOnly)-(.025*
EntryPrice(@,0,All,ThisTradeOnly))
```

Short Entry:

```
Close(@)[-1] XABOVE BHI(@,Sim,20,2)[-1]
AND Close(@)[-1] < MA(@,Sim,75)[-1]
```

Short Exit—Condition #1 set "Price" field to:

```
BMA(@,Sim,20)[-1]
```

Short Exit—Condition #2 set "Price" field to:

```
EntryPrice(@,0,All,ThisTradeOnly)+(.025* EntryPrice(@,0,All,
ThisTradeOnly))
```

Table 4.5 presents the backtested results from December 31, 1992, to December 31, 2002, for this system on our mean reversion portfolio.

As expected, the average duration of trades, time percentage in the market, and P:MD were all reduced considerably when compared with RSI extremes. This is because our mean reversion Bollinger band system exited at the 20-day moving average instead of holding trades longer to profit from the anticipated resumption of the longer-term trend. This same factor was also instrumental in the improvement of this system's winning trade percentage.

TABLE 4.5 Bollinger bands with 200–day moving average filter and 2.5% stop.

Asset	Profit	# Trades	# Days	Max Draw	MDD	MCL	P:MD	P:L Ratio	%W	Time %
ES	6192	36	5	−8239	680	3	0.75	1.39	66.67	6.43
IEURUSD	530	33	9	−8801	1468	2	0.06	1.02	66.67	10.27
IEURJPY	−9691	35	8	−20200	2426	5	−0.48	0.75	57.14	10.08
IEURCHF	14787	44	9	−4068	396	2	3.63	2.41	81.82	13.77
IEURCAD	7099	33	7	−14885	1037	3	0.48	1.17	69.70	7.23
IAUDCAD	17033	33	9	−3813	703	1	4.47	2.76	78.79	9.54
ICADJPY	1496	46	8	−10464	1467	3	0.14	1.05	65.22	12.31
IGBPAUD	20102	40	8	−10433	549	3	1.93	1.44	6.50	10.08
IGBPCHF	−6442	34	9	−22436	2391	3	−0.29	0.83	61.76	10.46
Totals	**51106**	**334**	**8**	**−26170**	**1780**	**4**	**1.95**	**1.44**	**68.26**	**10.20**

Note: All trade summaries include $100 round-turn trade deductions for slippage and commissions. Data source: CQG, Inc.

NONDIRECTIONALLY BIASED MEAN REVERSION SYSTEMS

Thus far we have examined only trend-following mean reversion systems. In reality, most mean reversion traders have no bias against countertrend trading. Thus, now I offer some nondirectionally biased mean reversion trading systems.

Bollinger Bands with ADX Filter

Although I am certain that there are instances in which ADX improves the performance of trend-following systems, in general I have found greater success with this indicator as a filter for mean reversion systems. Here we take the mean reversion Bollinger band system previously used and replace the 200-day moving average filter with ADX. This removes the directional or trend-following bias and replaces it with a filter that is intended to ensure a nontrending market condition.

In addition, as opposed to exiting with profits at the 20-day moving average, this system will exit based on a percentage of the asset's value at the time of trade initiation. Because certain assets are more volatile than others, we will set both the stop loss and profit exits at 2.5 percent of entry level for the E-mini S&P 500 and Japanese yen crosses. All other instruments will use a 1.25 percent move as the exit criteria.

Using CQG, the programming code for a Bollinger bands mean reversion system with ADX filter is written in this way:

Long Entry:

```
Close(@)[-1] XBELOW BLO(@,Sim,20,2)[-1] AND ADX(@,9)[-1] < 20
```

Long Exit—Condition #1 set "Price" field to:

```
EntryPrice(@,0,All,ThisTradeOnly)+(.0125* EntryPrice(@,0,All,
ThisTradeOnly))
```

Long Exit—Condition #2 set "Price" field to:

```
EntryPrice(@,0,All,ThisTradeOnly)-(.0125* EntryPrice(@,0,All,
ThisTradeOnly))
```

Short Entry:

```
Close(@)[-1] XABOVE BHI(@,Sim,20,2)[-1] AND ADX(@,9)[-1] < 20
```

Short Exit—Condition #1 set "Price" field to:

```
EntryPrice(@,0,All,ThisTradeOnly)-(.0125*
EntryPrice(@,0,All,ThisTradeOnly))
```

Short Exit—Condition #2 set "Price" field to:

```
EntryPrice(@,0,All,ThisTradeOnly)+(.0125* EntryPrice(@,0,All,
ThisTradeOnly))
```

Table 4.6 presents the backtested results from December 31, 1992, to December 31, 2002, for our mean reversion portfolio.

Notice that the elimination of the trend-following filter resulted in a deterioration of overall performance in virtually every category. (Compare Tables 4.5 and 4.6.) Although this is not always the case, most trend-following mean reversion systems do outperform their nondirectionally biased counterparts.

Slow Stochastics Extremes with Commodity Channel Index Filter

This mean reversion system initiates trades whenever both the slow stochastics and commodity channel index (CCI) indicators achieve extreme overbought or oversold levels. Exits occur when slow stochastics retreats from these unsustainable extremes or the failsafe stop loss level is triggered.

Using CQG, the programming code for our slow stochastics mean re-

TABLE 4.6 Bollinger bands with ADX filter, 1.25–2.5% stop loss, and profits exits.

Asset	Profit	# Trades	# Days	Max Draw	MDD	MCL	P:MD	P:L Ratio	%W	Time %
ES	−4336	20	9	−7480	1634	3	−0.58	0.68	45.00	6.56
IEURUSD	−2507	18	6	−7535	1922	3	−0.33	0.80	50.00	3.19
IEURJPY	17424	20	11	−9588	627	2	1.82	1.78	65.00	7.31
IEURCHF	7561	19	25	−8450	2002	3	0.89	1.50	63.16	17.43
IEURCAD	−534	19	5	−8792	1811	2	−0.06	0.97	52.63	2.88
IAUDCAD	−574	32	5	−6074	2451	4	−0.24	0.92	53.12	4.58
ICADJPY	−810	25	14	−10146	1275	4	−0.08	0.97	52.00	12.19
IGBPAUD	8524	16	5	−3187	794	2	3.37	1.96	76.47	2.30
IGBPCHF	−1128	22	8	−9021	2358	3	−0.12	0.94	50.00	5.85
Totals	**23620**	**191**	**9.7**	**−14741**	**779**	**5**	**1.60**	**1.13**	**55.62**	**7.00**

Note: All trade summaries include $100 round-turn trade deductions for slippage and commissions. Data source: CQG, Inc.

version system with CCI filter and 1.5 percent stop loss is written in this way:

Long Entry:

```
SSD(@,14,Smo,3,Smo,3)[-1] XBELOW 15 AND CCI(@,10) [-1] < -100
```

Long Exit—Condition #1:

```
SSD(@,14,Smo,3,Smo,3)[-1] XABOVE 30
```

Long Exit—Condition #2 set "Price" field to:

```
EntryPrice(@,0,All,ThisTradeOnly)-(.015*EntryPrice(@,0,All,
ThisTradeOnly))
```

Short Entry:

```
SSD(@,14,Smo,3,Smo,3)[-1] XABOVE 85 AND CCI(@,10)[-1] > 100
```

Short Exit—Condition #1:

```
SSD(@,14,Smo,3,Smo,3)[-1] XBELOW 70
```

Short Exit—Condition #2 set "Price" field to:

```
EntryPrice(@,0,All,ThisTradeOnly)+(.015* EntryPrice(@,0,All,
ThisTradeOnly))
```

Table 4.7 presents the backtested results from December 31, 1992, to December 31, 2002, for our mean reversion portfolio.

Here again we see marked deterioration of performance when compared to the trend-following mean reversion systems.

Slow Stochastics Extremes with CCI Filter and Time Exit

In many ways, mean reversion systems are polar opposites of their trend-following counterparts. With trend-following systems we let our profits run and relied on so-called outliers to compensate for our low percentage of winning trades. Inexorably linked to this concept of letting profits run is a prohibition against exiting trades due to the length of a trade's duration.

By contrast, with mean reversion systems, we can in some instances improve overall performance through the addition of a time-based exit criterion. Although in general I favor trading systems with the fewest parameters possible while still maintaining profitability, mean reversion traders should consider the introduction of time-based exits.[1]

TABLE 4.7 Slow stoachastics extremes with CCI filter and time exit.

Asset	Profit	# Trades	# Days	Max Draw	MDD	MCL	P:MD	P:L Ratio	%W	Time %
ES	−2048	36	9	−10840	2255	5	−0.19	0.90	44.44	10.96
IEURUSD	747	35	7	−11294	1549	4	0.07	1.03	54.29	8.12
IEURJPY	21675	40	8	−14852	1070	5	1.46	1.53	47.50	10.39
IEURCHF	−6516	21	10	−8870	2590	3	−0.73	0.43	52.38	7.66
IEURCAD	−930	35	8	−13858	1642	5	−0.07	0.98	45.71	9.03
IAUDCAD	5498	30	8	−10628	1715	3	0.52	1.33	56.67	8.23
ICADJPY	2380	36	7	−6742	1087	4	0.35	1.10	50.00	8.77
IGBPAUD	−7268	33	7	−12590	973	4	−0.58	0.80	51.52	8.23
IGBPCHF	5200	30	8	−15852	2014	7	0.33	1.18	50.00	8.04
Totals	**18738**	**296**	**7.9**	**−40490**	**1947**	**8**	**0.46**	**1.06**	**50.00**	**8.94**

Note: All trade summaries include $100 round-turn trade deductions for slippage and commissions. Data source: CQG, Inc.

Using CQG, the programming code for our slow stochastics mean reversion system with CCI filter, 1.5 percent stop loss, and 15-day time exit is written in this way:

Add This Third Condition to Both Long and Short Exits:

```
BarsSinceEntry(@,0,All,ThisTradeOnly) > 14
```

Table 4.8 presents the backtested results from December 31, 1992, to December 31, 2002, for our mean reversion portfolio.

TABLE 4.8 Slow stochastics extremes with CCI filter and time exit (shorter time frames).

Asset	Profit	# Trades	# Days	Max Draw	MDD	MCL	P:MD	P:L Ratio	%W	Time %
ES	2161	39	7	−6630	2230	5	0.33	1.12	43.59	9.45
IEURUSD	747	35	7	−11294	1539	4	0.07	1.03	54.29	8.15
IEURJPY	21525	40	8	−15002	1465	5	1.43	1.52	47.50	10.35
IEURCHF	−7306	20	10	−9660	2580	3	−0.74	0.40	55.00	7.22
IEURCAD	−510	35	8	−13573	1470	5	−0.04	0.99	44.12	8.92
IAUDCAD	5058	30	8	−11068	1719	3	0.46	1.30	56.67	8.23
ICADJPY	2380	36	7	−6742	1077	4	0.35	1.10	50.00	8.81
IGBPAUD	−6270	33	7	−12590	875	4	−0.50	0.82	51.52	8.12
IGBPCHF	5200	30	8	−15852	2014	7	0.33	1.18	50.00	8.04
Totals	**22985**	**298**	**7.7**	**−40490**	**1947**	**8**	**0.57**	**1.09**	**49.81**	**8.72**

Note: Results include a deduction of $100 per round-turn trade for slippage on daily time frame and $75 per round-turn for shorter time frames. Data source: CQG, Inc.

As expected, the most obvious points in our comparison of these results with Table 4.7 is the reduction of average trade duration and the system's time percentage in the market. In addition, the system did enjoy a modest improvement in P:MD.

PSYCHOLOGICAL PROFILE OF AN INTERMEDIATE-TERM MEAN REVERSION TRADER

Iron-Willed Discipline

Gain the Discipline to Fade the Crowd To succeed as mean reversion traders, traders have to overcome many psychological obstacles: crowd psychology, media hype, and the direction of recent price action. All of these particular demons can be boiled down to one basic personality prerequisite: discipline. Without the discipline (and courage) to fade recent price action, we will forever remain paralyzed with fear, unable to initiate the trades generated by our systems.

As a particular trading opportunity disappears and the market reverts to its mean, paralysis often turns into regret and determination to act the next time that a similar opportunity arises. Of course our next opportunity is accompanied by the same media hype, and bearish or bullish news, making it almost as difficult to overcome the paralysis as our previous attempts.

Oftentimes the next phase of our maturation as a mean reversion trader results in the manifestation of a form of the perfect trader syndrome. We now have the experience to recognize that these strategies do succeed, but we still lack the courage, discipline, and maturity to take the signals generated by our systems. Instead we attempt to outthink the system by placing entry orders at a point, which (if filled) would entail lower risk and higher reward.

In reality, this fine-tuning of our system is a modified version of the same trader paralysis that prevented us from taking the mean reversion signals in the first place. In most cases, the fine-tuning results in a filtering out of the majority of our system's winning trades and entry into all of its losers.

A number of techniques exist to aid with this problem. It is quite unpleasant to stand alone against what the majority believes to be a prudent course of action. However, it is important to remember that the crowd is usually wrong at temporarily unsustainable market extremes. We must train ourselves to associate that fear and the temptation to wait with lost opportunities and to associate the anxiety of taking the trading signals with success and profitability. As with trend trading, here again we must train ourselves to do something that feels uncomfortable and unnatural. Making money is not easy, and the market usually rewards us for doing that which is most difficult.

Regarding the perfect trader syndrome or the tendency to fine-tune entry points, we must remind ourselves that the strength of these systems is their high winning percentages. As a result, the filtering out of the majority of trades to minimize risk and increase reward will:

- Always reduce an already small number of trading opportunities
- Almost always worsen our win/loss ratio
- Usually transform moderately successful and robust systems into losers

Gain and Maintain the Discipline to Exit with Losses   It is extremely satisfying to buy low and sell high, and we all like to be right more often than we are wrong. Yet without the discipline to exit with losses when dictated by our system, one bad trade will end our career as a speculator. As the same can be said for trend trading systems, why do I place such a strong emphasis on the point here? Because these systems invariably will stop us out with relatively large losses, and it is very tempting to abandon discipline regarding stop losses when the losses are large relative to average profits. Acceptance of such losses means that we will have to enjoy quite a few profitable trades before experiencing a new peak in account equity.

In addition, because we are fading temporarily unsustainable extremes at the trade's outset, often our stops will be triggered near the ultimate high or low of the market's move. Inexperienced mean reversion traders find the temptation to abandon stop order discipline almost irresistible.

To help with this problem, look at the net profit column in Table 3.9 and remember that every one of these trades was initiated when the market achieved a statistically unsustainable overbought or oversold condition. Furthermore, a significant portion of the profits generated by every table in Chapter 3 was at the expense of traders in search of a bottom or top.

Successful mean reversion traders are not trying to catch bottoms and tops; instead, they are attempting to capitalize on a temporarily unsustainable level of euphoria or panic. Such trades have a high probability of success, as illustrated by their superior win/loss ratios. However, if the market continues trending in the direction of what we previously believed was an unsustainable move, then our assumptions regarding the trend were wrong, and the only acceptable action is immediate exiting of the trade.

Uncomfortable with More Losers than Winners and Unwilling to Withstand a Large Number of Consecutive Losses

There is nothing wrong with a trader who has difficulty handling a small winning percentage or large number of consecutive losses. The point here is to make an honest assessment of strengths and weaknesses, then employ a trading strategy that capitalizes on these traits.

With discipline, patience, and prudent price risk management, I believe traders can enjoy success utilizing a wide variety of strategies including those that have good win/loss ratios. However, everything is a trade-off, and the sacrifice endured to enjoy solid win/loss percentages are that most mean reversion systems yield smaller rates of return vis-à-vis risk and experience larger per trade losses relative to winners.

Readers should ask themselves: Would I prefer a large winning percentage while occasionally enduring a loss that forfeits a significant portion of accumulated profits, or am I willing to endure multiple consecutive losses as long as they are much smaller than my profitable trades? The answer to this question will enable readers to determine whether they are better suited to trend or mean reversion trading.

Unyielding Patience

A subtler yet potentially more destructive disadvantage in executing intermediate-term mean reversion systems are the smaller number of trading opportunities. Fewer opportunities suggest a mastery of patience, and without this ability to wait on the sidelines for unsustainable market extremes to manifest themselves, we are destined to settle for higher risk/lower probability opportunities.

Readers should review Table 4.8's "number of trades" column to assess whether they have the patience required to execute these systems. Then ask: Do I have the patience to wait for the 30 trading opportunities that occur throughout the typical trading year? Am I okay with being out of the market around 91 percent of the time?

No Vacations from the Markets

Although the systems included in this chapter generated trading signals on a closing basis and traders therefore aren't tied to the computer screen throughout the trading day, implicitly linked to the concept of patience and fewer trading opportunities is the fact that when these rare moments of unsustainable market action occur, we must be on hand to capitalize on them.

CHAPTER 5

Short-Term Systems

A Matter of Quick Mindedness

Do not dwell in the past, do not dream of the future, concentrate the mind on the present moment.

—The Buddha

FADING THE LOSING SYSTEM

Another myth of system development is that the discovery of a losing system is a method of successful system development. This myth assumes that the fading of every losing trade would yield a profit. The main flaw in this thinking is that fading marginally unsuccessful systems produces another losing system once realistic commissions and slippage are deducted from results. The other, subtler flaw in this reasoning stems from the fact that we must be able to weather the worst peak-to-valley equity drawdowns inherent in fading the losing system. Doing so usually entails the introduction of a fail-safe stop loss, which, in some cases, will turn a marginally profitable system into an overall loser.

LIQUIDITY AND VOLATILITY

Although the benefits of diversification among various asset classes are indisputable (as illustrated by the tables in Chapter 3), when we shift our time frames from long or intermediate term to short term, the trading of most assets becomes impractical. There are two basic reasons behind the failure of various assets in short-term systems trading: illiquidity and lack of volatility.

Illiquidity in the context of short-term systems trading means that the total net profits generated by a system are insufficient to compensate for the wide intraday slippage (or bid/ask spreads) plus commissions of a particular trading vehicle. Because the average per-trade profit for a day trading system will necessarily be significantly smaller than trades held for one to six months, the deduction of $100 for slippage and commissions often turns a successful long-term methodology into a losing short-term strategy. Consequently most trading instruments are not liquid enough to compensate for the loss of a typical bid/ask spread plus commissions. As a result, unless traders are market makers or own a seat on the exchange floor, intraday bid/ask spreads and commissions will automatically disqualify the vast majority of assets from implementation as successful short-term trading systems.

Inexorably tied to the concept of a lower net profit per trade is the prohibition against assets that lack superior intraday volatility. Although many vehicles provide traders with an adequate speed and magnitude of price movement to compensate for slippage and commissions on long- or intermediate-term trading systems, very few remain profitable when the time frame is shortened to signals generated by 5- or 15-minute bars.

To illustrate the effects of slippage, commissions and lack of intraday volatility, I include a study of the trend-following moving average convergence/divergence (MACD) system showcased in Chapter 3 on one of the best trending and more volatile vehicles, IEURUSD, or spot euro currency versus U.S. dollar (see Table 5.1). Notice how this system's profitability deteriorates as the time frames are shortened. (Although the system was marginally profitable over the 30-minute time frame, I feel this was an aberration since the 60- and 15-minute time frames showed losses).

Although market liquidity and volatility are constantly changing, as of this writing, I feel that, in general, only the assets shown in Table 5.2 should be considered for swing and day trading time frames and types of trading

TABLE 5.1 DM–euro/U.S. dollar with MACD over various time frames.

Time Frame	Total Net Profit	P:MD	Data History	# Days
Daily	21280	0.81	12/31/93–12/31/03	145.0
120 Minutes	3545	0.10	3/28/00–1/21/04	11.5
60 Minutes	−6715	−0.40	10/11/01–1/21/04	5.4
30 Minutes	3950	0.27	12/4/02–1/21/04	2.9
15 Minutes	−7595	−0.46	7/3/03–1/21/04	1.5
5 Minutes	−5120	−0.53	11/19/03–1/21/04	0.5

Note: results include a deduction of $100 per round-turn trade for slippage on daily time frame and $75 per round-turn for shorter time frames. Data source: CQG, Inc.

systems. Please note that I have examined U.S.-based trading only; this table does not reflect assets traded on European or Asian exchanges.

Table 5.2 introduces three new symbols: ND, SP, and US. ND is the symbol for the Nasdaq 100 index, and SP is the symbol for the full-sized S&P 500 contract, which is 250 times the index (as opposed to the E-mini S&P 500 contract, which was 50 times the index). Why include ND and SP here instead of continuing to use ES as in Chapters 3 and 4? The primary reason is that we need the superior volatility of these instruments to compensate for the lower amount of our average per-trade profits. (For this same reason we have abandoned TY in favor of US, the symbol for CBOT pit session continuation T-bonds.)

We excluded US, ND, and SP from Chapters 3 and 4 because we did not want the volatility of a single asset to dominate our backtested portfolio results. Because the majority of this chapter's backtested results showcase equity indices only, portfolio diversification is no longer a consideration.

Although we could have shown the combined results of ND and SP, I felt that the correlations between these two assets were too high and so have decided to work primarily with the Nasdaq 100 index due to its superior volatility (although we do employ the S&P 500 for the 15- and 5-minute bar time frames).

BACKTESTED RESULTS

From Table 5.2 we see that only the equity indices demonstrated consistent profitability in shorter time frames. Consequently, I have decided to use only the Nasdaq 100 index in most of our studies of short-term trading vehicles. Because only corporations, banks, and institutional brokerage houses run 24-hour trading desks, I will assume that our T-bond trades occur only during CBOT pit trading hours (8:20 A.M.–3:00 P.M.) and will use cash market trading hours for equity index trades (9:30 A.M.–4:00 P.M.).

This reduction of trading hours to "day session" eliminates the assumption of a 24-hour trading desk while simultaneously ensuring superior

TABLE 5.2 Assets and time frames: historical tendencies.

Time Frame	Asset	System Type	Trading Hours
120 minutes	FX majors	Trending	24 hours
120 minutes	US	Trending	Day session
120 minutes	ND, SP, ES	Mean reverting	Day session
60, 30, 15, and 5 minutes	ND, SP	Mean reverting	Day Session

Note: results include a deduction of $100 per round-turn trade for slippage on daily time frame and $75 per round-turn for shorter time frames. Data source: CQG, Inc.

liquidity and realistic slippage/commissions deductions. Although this means that we will miss opportunities to initiate or exit trades on the 24-hour electronic market, I believe that a robust short-term system should be able to catch a significant portion of trading opportunities.

One positive trade-off that somewhat compensates for the loss of the vast majority of trading vehicles is a reduction in our slippage and commissions assumptions. Because we are now trading only the most liquid instruments and only during the trading hours of their greatest liquidity, we can reduce commissions and slippage deductions from $100 to $75 per round-turn trade. Although this sounds like a ridiculously small improvement, because these systems generate so many trades over a year's time, it actually does make a moderately positive impact on our bottom line.

SWING TRADING WITH 2-HOUR BARS

Various market participants define swing trading in different ways. For the sake of clarity and consistency we will define swing trading as trades typically held for more than 1 and less than 10 trading days. The intermediate-term mean reversion systems highlighted in Chapter 4 had an average duration of 8 to 20 trading days. Therefore, swing trades bridge the gap between intermediate-term and day trading systems. Some market participants use the term *swing trading* to designate nondirectionally biased mean reversion strategies; because I define the term based on this purely time-driven criteria, we will examine trend-following, trend-following mean reversion, and nondirectionally biased mean reversion swing trading systems.

Trend-Following Swing Trading: Channel Breakout

To examine a typical trend-following swing trading system, we will modify the channel breakout system used in Chapter 3 by changing the entry criteria from 20- to 15-day highs or lows and reducing the exit condition to the violation of 8-day highs or lows. This shifts our original system from a stop and reverse to one that allows for neutrality during sideways market action. In addition, to ensure that these trades remain "short term" in duration, we have added a time-driven exit criteria that will be triggered on trades held beyond 7.5 days. (See Chapter 4, "Time-Driven Exit Filters," for the programming code.)

Because we only trade T-bonds during their day session, whereas the euro/U.S. dollar generates trades 24 hours a day, we need to equalize our trading system's parameters by converting the number of 2-hour bars per trading day for both assets as illustrated in Table 5.3.

TABLE 5.3 Example of equalization of trading days for pit versus 24-hour assets.

Bars per Trading Day	Number of Trading Days	Number of 2-hour Bars
4	15	60
12	15	180

Data source: CQG, Inc.

Notice in Table 5.3 that an equal number of trading days means an unequal number of bars (e.g., 15 days in T-bonds is 60 2-hour bars as opposed to 180 bars for IEURUSD). Although this may seem counterintuitive, an examination of the average duration of trades and percentage of time in the market columns from Table 5.4 proves it is the preferable method of comparing pit session assets to those traded over a 24-hour time frame.

Furthermore, because the euro trades around the clock and we trade T-bonds only during local pit trading hours, the lengths of our data histories are different. (IEURUSD runs only from March 28, 2000, to January 30, 2004, whereas CBOT data for continuation pit session T-bonds goes back to December 30, 1998.) Consequently, the combined portfolio results for the two assets have been omitted. We can, however, generate average annualized results for this system for both assets and then compare these to our longer-term trading systems. Annualizing our total net profits for IEURUSD equates to roughly $5,006.25 per year, whereas T-bonds yielded a more modest $2,490 (although we will still retain the maximum drawdowns shown in Table 5.4).

Notice that both assets compare quite favorably with the majority of component-based results generated throughout Chapter 3. In fact, only the annualized profit to maximum drawdown (P:MD) of the Japanese yen proved consistently comparable to those generated in Table 5.4. This suggests that an improved rate of return at least somewhat compensates for the lack of diversification inherent in implementation of short-term trading systems.

TABLE 5.4 Channel breakout with 15–day entry and 8–day exit plus 7.5–day time exit.

Asset	Profit	# Trades	# Days	Max Draw	MDD	MCL	P:MD	P:L Ratio	%W	Time %
US	12450	89	7.3	−12237	323	4	1.02	1.24	52.81	62.59
IEURUSD	20025	95	6.9	−7840	399	4	2.55	1.34	51.58	59.86

Note: results include a deduction of $100 per round-turn trade for slippage on daily time frame and $75 per round-turn for shorter time frames. Data source: CQG, Inc.

Swing Trading with 2-Hour Bars: Mean Reversion Systems

Here we will work with two of the mean reversion systems highlighted in Chapter 4: one trend-following mean reversion system and one nondirectionally biased mean reversion system. Both systems will use 120-minute bar charts on the Nasdaq 100 index. The data displayed includes history from November 30, 1998, to January 30, 2004.

Relative Strength Index Extremes with 400-Hour Moving Average Filter

Relative strength index (RSI) extremes with 400-hour moving average filter is the same trend-following mean reversion system that generated the best performance of those used throughout Chapter 4 and uses the same CQG code.

Table 5.5 presents results of this system for the Nasdaq 100 index (day session only).

As expected, because this system exits trades near the mean, our average trade duration and percentage of time in the market have decreased when compared with the trend-following swing trading system results shown in Table 5.4. What is most surprising is the system's unusually poor win/loss ratio. This is in stark contrast to the results shown in Chapter 4 and is a direct result of this asset's extraordinarily high volatility.

Slow Stochastics Extremes with CCI filter and Time Exit

Here again we revisit a mean reversion system that was originally introduced in Chapter 4. Unlike the RSI extremes with moving average filter, this system has no directional bias.

Table 5.6 presents the results of this system for the Nasdaq 100 index (day session only).

As in Chapter 4, here again the removal of the trend-following prerequisite led to a deterioration in profit to maximum drawdown as well as to a

TABLE 5.5   RSI extremes with 400-hour moving average filter.

Asset	Profit	# Trades	# Days	Max Draw	MDD	MCL	P:MD	P:L Ratio	%W	Time %
ND	105027	138	2.75	−76043	627	5	1.38	1.20	36.23	16.76

Note: results include a deduction of $100 per round-turn trade for slippage on daily time frame and $75 per round-turn for shorter time frames. Data source: CQG, Inc.

TABLE 5.6 Slow stochastics extremes with CCI filter and 30-hour time exit.

Asset	Profit	# Trades	# Days	Max Draw	MDD	MCL	P:MD	P:L Ratio	%W	Time %
ND	70093	110	1.5	−69336	954	9	1.01	1.33	41.82	4.27

Note: results include a deduction of $100 per round-turn trade for slippage on daily time frame and $75 per round-turn for shorter time frames. Data source: CQG, Inc.

significant improvement in percentage of winning trades. To reiterate, slow stochastics extremes enjoyed a higher winning percentage because it exits trades as soon as the market reverts to its mean. By contrast, RSI extremes held trades on average for almost twice as long to capitalize on the reassertion of the "longer-term" trend.

MEAN REVERSION SYSTEMS USING 60-MINUTE BARS

As a general rule, the longer the time frame chosen, the greater diversity of profitable trading systems available to system traders. Here we will showcase three trading systems using 60-minute bar charts on the Nasdaq 100 index. The data displayed includes history from November 30, 1998, to January 30, 2004.

RSI Extremes with 200-Hour Moving Average Filter

Table 5.7 presents the results of this same trend-following mean reversion system for the 60-minute time frame.

Despite increases in maximum drawdown and maximum consecutive losses, a comparison of Tables 5.5 and 5.7 shows considerable overall improvements for this system's performance over the shorter time frame. Especially noteworthy were improvements in percentages of winning trades as well as the profit to maximum drawdown ratios. Although such superior performance is indisputable, I would not throw away the 2-hour time frame

TABLE 5.7 RSI extremes with 200-hour moving average filter.

Asset	Profit	# Trades	# Days	Max Draw	MDD	MCL	P:MD	P:L Ratio	%W	Time %
ND	115647	214	1.75	−77166	234	7	1.50	1.17	44.39	20.04

Note: results include a deduction of $100 per round-turn trade for slippage on daily time frame and $75 per round-turn for shorter time frames. Data source: CQG, Inc.

in favor of 60-minute bars. In general, as shown in Table 5.1, performance of mechanical trading systems tends to deteriorate as time frames are shortened.

NONDIRECTIONALLY BIASED MEAN REVERSION SYSTEMS

Seven-Period Reversal

The seven-period reversal works because it generates trades only when markets are extremely overbought or oversold. For example, sell signals are initiated only when markets can move consistently higher for seven consecutive bars and then reverse direction on the most recent bar. This strategy differs from the mean reversion systems discussed so far in that it generates buy or sell signals only when the market has reversed its short-term trend (at least during the most recent bar).

Although there are many successful ways to exit this system, I will employ a seven-period reversal criteria along with profit targets and fail-safe stop loss exits set to 1 percent of entry price.

Long Entry:

```
Close(@)[-8] > Close(@)[-7] AND
Close(@)[-7] > Close(@)[-6] AND
Close(@)[-6] > Close(@)[-5] AND
Close(@)[-5] > Close(@)[-4] AND
Close(@)[-4] > Close(@)[-3] AND
Close(@)[-3] > Close(@)[-2]
AND Close(@)[-2] < Close(@)[-1]
```

Long Exit—Condition #1:

```
Close(@)[-7] < Close(@)[-6] AND
Close(@)[-6] < Close(@)[-5] AND
Close(@)[-5] < Close(@)[-4] AND
Close(@)[-4] < Close(@)[-3] AND
Close(@)[-3] < Close(@)[-2]
AND Close(@)[-2] < Close(@)[-1]
```

Long Exit—Condition #2 set "Price" field to:

```
EntryPrice(@,0,All,ThisTradeOnly)+(.01*
EntryPrice(@,0,All,ThisTradeOnly))
```

Long Exit—Condition #3 set "Price" field to:

```
EntryPrice(@,0,All,ThisTradeOnly)-(.01*
EntryPrice(@,0,All,ThisTradeOnly))
```

For short entry, along with short exit codes for condition #1, simply reverse all greater than and less than signs. For short exit conditions #2 and #3, just reverse the plus and minus signs.

Once again, a comparison of Tables 5.7 and 5.8 shows that the elimination of our trend-following filter resulted in a deterioration of profit to maximum drawdown (P:MD) ratios. Of course, as in Chapter 4, this also improved our win/loss ratio and reduced the number of consecutive losses endured.

Perhaps most significant of all was the dramatic reduction of the worst drawdown. Although the trend-following mean reversion system was more robust in theory, its large maximum drawdown meant that the vast majority of smaller trading accounts would not have benefited from its superior P:MD.

RSI Crossover

This system generates long entry signals whenever the 14-period RSI was less than 25 two bars ago and then crosses above 25 on the prior bar. (Short entries are generated whenever RSI was above 75 two bars ago and then crossed below 75 on the prior bar.) Like the seven-period reversal method, this system generates signals only when the short-term trending action has reversed (thereby suggesting a reversion to the mean is under way).

Long Entry:

```
RSI(@,14)[-2] < 25 AND RSI(@,14)[-1] XABOVE 25
```

Long Exit—Condition #1 set "Price" field to:

```
EntryPrice(@,0,All,ThisTradeOnly)+(.03*
EntryPrice(@,0,All,ThisTradeOnly))
```

TABLE 5.8 Seven-bar reversal with 1% profit and stop exit.

Asset	Profit	# Trades	# Days	Max Draw	MDD	MCL	P:MD	P:L Ratio	%W	Time %
ND	55696	166	0.75	–43783	682	5	1.27	1.30	48.8	5.44

Note: results include a deduction of $100 per round-turn trade for slippage on daily time frame and $75 per round-turn for shorter time frames. Data source: CQG, Inc.

Long Exit—Condition #2 set "Price" field to:

```
EntryPrice(@,0,All,ThisTradeOnly)-(.01*
EntryPrice(@,0,All,ThisTradeOnly))
```

Short Entry:

```
RSI(@,14)[-2] > 75 AND RSI(@,14)[-1] XBELOW 75
```

For short exits, simply reverse the plus and minus signs used for long exits.

Notice how Table 5.8's identical profit target and fail-safe stop loss resulted in its enjoyment of a higher winning percentage and smaller number of maximum consecutive losses than Table 5.9.

MEAN REVERSION SYSTEMS USING 30-MINUTE BARS

The data displayed for the 30-minute bar time frame include history from February 14, 2000, to January 30, 2004.

RSI Extremes with 100-Hour Moving Average Filter

Table 5.10 shows that one of our most successful and robust trading systems up until this point has failed miserably in this shorter time frame.

TABLE 5.9 RSI crossover with 3% profit exit and 1% stop.

Asset	Profit	# Trades	# Days	Max Draw	MDD	MCL	P:MD	P:L Ratio	%W	Time %
ND	51092	141	0.9	−46647	700	14	1.10	1.25	26.24	5.61

Note: results include a deduction of $100 per round-turn trade for slippage on daily time frame and $75 per round-turn for shorter time frames. Data source: CQG, Inc.

TABLE 5.10 RSI extremes with 100-hour moving average filter an 2.5% stop.

Asset	Profit	# Trades	# Days	Max Draw	MDD	MCL	P:MD	P:L Ratio	%W	Time %
ND	−62385	275	1.125	−117578	860	8	−0.53	0.92	49.82	32.61

Note: results include a deduction of $100 per round-turn trade for slippage on daily time frame and $75 per round-turn for shorter time frames. Data source: CQG, Inc.

Whenever a trading system shifts so dramatically from profitability, we need to ask why.

One possible answer could be that the fixed costs and smaller per-trade profits means that this system was destined to fail over shorter time frames. This deterioration as time frames are shortened was exemplified in our examination of IEURUSD with MACD in Table 5.1. These same factors may be the underlying cause of the failure occurring in Table 5.10; to determine if this is true, we must compare the conditions in Table 5.1 to those in Table 5.10.

A distinct difference between MACD and RSI extremes was that MACD's entry and exit conditions were all based on indicators (exponential moving averages) that automatically adapted to whatever time frame was being traded. By contrast, one of the exit conditions in RSI extremes was based on a static percentage value of the asset at the time of our trade's initiation. Since our profitable exit condition was based on the RSI indicator's achievement of a specific level (which, like MACD, adapted to our change of time frames) and our fail-safe stop-loss was based on the static 2.5 percent of contract value at the trade's initiation, this suggests the need to reduce the fail-safe stop-loss levels to compensate for declining volatility inherent in execution of this system over shorter time frames.

Therefore, it is reasonable to assume that this failure to adjust our stop-loss level as volatility contracted over the shorter time frame should have resulted in smaller profits and occasional large losses. In fact, a comparison of Tables 5.5, 5.7, and 5.10 demonstrates that as time frames were shortened, the winning percentages increased steadily and dramatically. This proves that the static 2.5 percent stop loss, which was robust enough for the 2-hour and 60-minute time frames, needs to be adjusted for shorter time frames.

Table 5.11 shows the results of employing the same RSI extremes systems with a smaller, 1.5 percent fail-safe stop. As expected, both the profit to maximum drawdown ratios as well as the win/loss ratios is now comparable with those seen in Table 5.7.

TABLE 5.11 RSI extremes with 100-hour moving average filter and 1.5% stop.

Asset	Profit	# Trades	# Days	Max Draw	MDD	MCL	P:MD	P:L Ratio	%W	Time %
ND	93635	336	0.875	−54215	273	12	1.73	1.14	38.99	30.14

Note: results include a deduction of $100 per round-turn trade for slippage on daily time frame and $75 per round-turn for shorter time frames. Data source: CQG, Inc.

RSI Crossover with Stops and Profit Exits Set to 1 Percent

All programming code for this system is the same as shown in the 60-minute time frame with the exception of long and short exit conditions #1, which have been reduced from 3 percent to 1 percent beyond entry price, thereby equalizing profit and stop-loss levels.

Although this system obviously produced drastically inferior results from its 60-minute bar counterpart, remember that it includes only four years' as opposed to five years' performance for the 120- and 60-minute bar systems. This raises several questions; first, why did we lose the data from 1999 when we shortened our time frame? Data vendors can store only a finite amount of history. Therefore, as time frames are shortened, the storage of an equal number of historical data bars will yield a smaller time frame of history. For example, as of this writing, CQG stores 15,000 bars, which is five years' worth of 60-minute bars but only four years' worth of 30-minute bars.

Would inclusion of 1999's data have improved performance for the 30-minute time frame in Table 5.12? Although it is reasonable to assume this to be the case since these systems were profitable overall, the fact that Table 5.1 showed deterioration over shorter time frames for a different asset on a negatively and/or uncorrelated (trend-following) system makes me reasonably confident that inclusion of 1999's performance would not have changed the overall pattern of declining P:MD as time frames are shortened.

The next question is how to generate comparable "synthetic" data histories through equalization of results to compensate for the loss of 1999 on our 30-minute systems. Although we can never know with certainty exactly how 1999 would have impacted the system's performance in this time frame, we can equalize our results to those generated by our 60-minute time frame by dividing each system's total net profit by the number of years displayed in its data history. For example, the annualized total net profit for Table 5.9 would be roughly $10,218.40, whereas the annualized total net profit for Table 5.12 was around $2,539.50. (As before, we should still assume the same maximum drawdowns for both tables.)

TABLE 5.12   RSI crossover with 1% stop loss and profit.

Asset	Profit	# Trades	# Days	Max Draw	MDD	MCL	P:MD	P:L Ratio	%W	Time %
ND	10158	204	0.9	−56738	601	12	0.18	1.03	25.00	18.92

Note: results include a deduction of $100 per round-turn trade for slippage on daily time frame and $75 per round-turn for shorter time frames. Data source: CQG, Inc.

15-MINUTE BAR SYSTEMS: RSI EXTREMES WITH 50-HOUR MOVING AVERAGE FILTER

The data displayed in Table 5.13 for the 15-minute bar time frame includes history from February 5, 2002, to January 30, 2004. Because our time frame was again shortened, we reduced our fail-safe stop-loss level to 1 percent of entry price for ND. In addition, because SP is less volatile than ND, we reduced its fail-safe stop loss to 0.5 percent of entry price.

Performance deterioration over this time frame was so dramatic that I had to include SP to show a profitable trading asset for our mechanical trading systems. Furthermore, such profits were achievable only with the trend-following mean reversion system, and even here the P:MD was only moderately successful. Although nondirectionally biased mean reversion systems can work with 15- and 5-minute bars, in general, I have found that mean reversion systems containing a trend-following filter tend to be the most robust over these time frames.

5-MINUTE BAR SYSTEMS: RSI EXTREMES WITH 16.67-HOUR MOVING AVERAGE FILTER

The data displayed in Table 5.14 for the 5-minute bar time frame includes history from June 25, 2003, to January 30, 2004.

When comparing the performance in Table 5.14 to that of Table 5.13, two notable improvements occurred as the time frames of our bars were shortened: the maximum number of consecutive losses and win/loss ratio for the system. This was a direct result of our maintaining the same RSI and percentage stop-loss parameters despite the shortening of time frames. Because mean reversion on shorter time frames requires a smaller magnitude of price movement, likelihood of mean reversion became greater vis-à-vis the probability of achieving the identical fail-safe stop level. As a result we saw improvements in win/loss ratio and consecutive losses as our P:MD dropped.

TABLE 5.13 RSI extremes with 50-hour moving average filter and 1% stop for ND; 0.5% stop for SP.

Asset	Profit	# Trades	# Days	Max Draw	MDD	MCL	P:MD	P:L Ratio	%W	Time %
SP	13869	316	0.4	−31608	365	11	0.44	1.05	37.34	29.14
ND	−9048	278	0.5	−27185	342	11	−0.33	0.96	42.81	30.08

Note: results include a deduction of $100 per round-turn trade for slippage on daily time frame and $75 per round-turn for shorter time frames. Data source: CQG, Inc.

TABLE 5.14 RSI extremes with 16.67-hour moving average filter and 1% stop for ND; 0.5% stop for SP.

Asset	Profit	# Trades	# Days	Max Draw	MDD	MCL	P:MD	P:L Ratio	%W	Time %
SP	3042	191	0.2	−11110	65	4	0.27	1.04	66.49	35.10
ND	−622	170	0.3	−11905	84	3	−0.04	0.99	67.06	34.11

Note: results include a deduction of $100 per round-turn trade for slippage on daily time frame and $75 per round-turn for shorter time frames. Data source: CQG, Inc.

PSYCHOLOGICAL PROFILE OF A SHORT-TERM TRADER

Because short-term traders must make so many decisions during a typical business day, they are among the most likely of the trading personality types to benefit from systematic trading during the initial phase of their careers. More means more—more decisions, more opportunities, and most of all, more stress. Mechanical trading systems eliminate the seat-of-your-pants stress normally synonymous with short-term and especially with day trading techniques.

Because mechanical day traders (in contrast to their discretionary counterparts) have quantified entry, exit, risk and (in most cases) reward, it transforms their modus operandi from fast thinking, fast reactions, and faster burnout into a virtually limitless life expectancy.

Short-term systems can be attractive when compared to intermediate or long-term trading alternatives. Remember that the P:MD shown for the euro in Table 5.4 was 2.55. This compares quite favorably with the top-performing assets throughout Chapters 3 and 4. As stated earlier, the trade-off is that the performance of these shorter-term systems deteriorates dramatically when the trading vehicles analyzed exclude the assets highlighted throughout this chapter. We gain an attractive annualized rate of return and P:MD, but we lose the ability to diversify among negatively and/or uncorrelated asset classes.

A subtler disadvantage is the labor-intensive nature of these systems. Adherence to the system suggests that traders are married to the screen during trading hours. By contrast, for the systems presented in Chapters 3 and 4, traders generally need to check their screens only once a day (usually at the close to determine if entry signals were triggered or stops required adjustment).

Although it is true that short-term traders need to monitor their screens on a continuous basis, since day traders have so many more opportunities, they can and should take vacations to recharge their batteries. Trend traders cannot take vacations to recharge because their sole method of compensating for inferior win/loss ratios lies in their ability to capitalize on the few large profitable trades that surface each year. Intermediate-term mean reversion traders also cannot enjoy vacations due to the infrequent occurrences of their high-probability trading signals.

In this chapter's title I used the term *quick-mindedness* to crystallize the personality trait needed for success as a swing or day trader. Because these traders are faced with intraday trading decisions, their ability to think on their feet and manage the stress inherent in making 2 to 20 snap judgments each day suggests mastery of a different skill set from their long- or intermediate-term counterparts.

Because day trading is more physically and psychologically demanding and draining than other types of trading, day traders are the most susceptible to burnout. Consequently, beyond my earlier suggestions of using a mechanical system to reduce stress and taking frequent vacations from the market to recharge mental batteries, the key to longevity as a short-term trader rests in the ability to have balance in life—physically, emotionally, mentally, and spiritually. (Although this concept of balance is applicable to intermediate- and long-term traders, it is an almost unwritten and immutable law for swing and day traders.) I say "almost" because we can train ourselves to do anything we set our minds to, and there are exceptions to every rule. Nevertheless, without proper rest, relaxation, exercise, and emotional support from family and friends, burnout is a high-probability occupational hazard for short-term traders.

Although people with this type of short-term trading personality can be trend traders, more typically they gravitate toward mean reversion trading and asset classes. Such traders have mastered many of the traits covered in Chapter 4—the ability to fade the crowd, media hype, and news—coupled with an ability to thrive in the midst of the near-constant activity that defines short-term trading. Typically they enjoy the intraday market action with its requirements of intense focus and concentration, and (if experienced and disciplined) can sometimes even achieve peace and stillness within the heart of chaos and ever-changing market prices.

CHAPTER 6

Knowing Oneself

How to Challenge Your Knowledge

To thine own self be true.

—William Shakespeare

TRADER PSYCHOLOGY: EVER THE SAME AND PERPETUALLY CHANGING

Successful trading in all its manifestations and time frames has one common characteristic: It is difficult to implement. Because buyers and sellers are always on opposite sides of a transaction, logic might lead us to believe that 50 percent of all traders should succeed. The odds are much worse because the essence of successful trading entails consistently doing the unnatural and uncomfortable thing.[1] The manifestation of successful trading will differ greatly depending on whether a person is following the trend or fading recent price action and depending on the trading time frame; irrespective of these particulars, traders always will be forced to fight natural inclinations toward comfort, security, impatience, perfection, fear, and greed.

Successful trend traders must train themselves to do what is unnatural and uncomfortable by selling recent lows and buying recent new highs, accepting more losers than winners, and letting profits run. Although mean reversion trading is in many ways the antithesis of trend trading, these participants too must train themselves to do what is unnatural and uncomfortable by going against the logic, hype, and propaganda of the crowd and fading the recent price action once it achieves temporarily unsustainable extremes.

In either instance, the process of reprogramming oneself away from the easy and comfortable trading decisions involves discipline, patience, flexibility, and a commitment to follow through on a plan of action irrespective of its difficulties and distractions.

TIME FRAMES, TRADING SYSTEMS, AND PERSONALITY TRAITS

Although there are almost infinite delineations of time frames and just as many variations of trading systems, I will use the systems and time frames mapped out in Chapter 3, Chapter 4, and Chapter 5 to examine different personality types and how these types naturally gravitate to particular time frames and strategies.

Many of the advantages and disadvantages of these categories overlap. Wherever possible throughout this chapter, however, I try to introduce unique and previously unexplored aspects of prerequisites for success in each trading methodology and time frame.

Long-term Trend-Following System Trading

Typical duration of trade: 5 to 10 months
Example: MACD

Advantages:
- Requires least attention to the markets.
- No intraday action required.
- Typically generates largest per-trade profits and enjoys the best profit to maximum drawdown ratios.
- Works with many negatively and/or uncorrelated asset classes.
- Because it entails the fewest decisions, it is often viewed as the least stressful of all mechanical trading strategies (assuming the trader does not find sitting on positions long term without reacting to short-term fluctuations stressful).

Disadvantages:
- Inactivity.
- Inability to capitalize on obvious short-term, event-driven (government reports, news events, etc.) countertrend opportunities.
- Requires overnight margin.
- Typically experiences poor win/loss ratios and a large number of consecutive losses.

- Often risks larger percentage of equity on a per-trade basis than shorter-term trading systems.
- Because the duration of trades is the longest, reliability of backtested system results is based on fewest occurrences. This makes statistical validity of certain portfolio results, such as maximum drawdown and maximum consecutive losses, more suspect (unless backtested data history is lengthened accordingly).
- Inability to capitalize on short or intermediate fluctuations in the market.

This problem can be countered, in part, by trading around core position. Trading around the core position entails holding a portion of the core position until the longer-term trend reverses while trading in and out of the remainder of the position to capitalize on short- or intermediate-term opportunities.

To execute this strategy successfully, capitalization must be sufficient. Use of multiple contracts in this manner is prudent only if it does not result in abandonment of prudent price risk management standards (as outlined in Chapter 8).

Trading around the core position often satisfies the psychological need to do something to earn a livelihood as traders. The Puritan work ethic suggests that we deserve wealth only if we sweat each day earning it. Although the extensive research required in formulation and rigorous testing of trading systems could be viewed as a fulfillment of this psychological prerequisite to deserve wealth, more often traders feel that activity in the markets is the only measure of having earned and therefore of deserving success.

Until we can convince our subconscious that inactivity is hard work and deserving of the reward of wealth, the strategy of trading around the core position can aid us in feeling psychologically worthy of success. Although this process will commonly result in relinquishing the noncore portion of the position during the acceleration phase of a trend, as long as we can make our peace with the high probability of the loss of our core position occurrence, the strategy is extremely beneficial in training us to stick with part of our position longer than we might otherwise be able to bear.

Intermediate to Long-Term Trend-Following Systems

Typical duration of trade: 6 weeks to 5 months
Example: Channel breakout

Advantages:
- Making fewer decisions than shorter-time frame traders usually equates to less stress (especially since intraday stress has been eliminated).

- Large per-trade profits.
- Works with many negatively and/or uncorrelated asset classes.
- Greater frequency of trades and shorter duration of trades than longer-term systems makes this time frame more palatable to "active" trend traders.
- Backtested results are more statistically significant than those of longer-term systems based on the same length of data history.

Disadvantages:

- As with the long-term trend-following systems, participation in this time frame usually means an inability to capitalize on obvious shorter-term, event-driven countertrend opportunities.
- Typically experiences poor win/loss ratios and a large number of consecutive losses.
- Positions require posting of overnight margin.
- Often risks larger percentage of equity on a per-trade basis than short-term system traders.
- As with all trend-following systems, it requires the ability to buy recent highs, sell recent lows, and relinquish a significant portion of unrealized profits.

Intermediate-Term Trend Following

Typical duration of trade: 2 to 8 weeks
Examples: Moving average crossovers, Bollinger bands, DMI

Advantages:

- Greater sensitivity to trend changes often means this time frame has the ability to participate in newly developing trends quicker and sometimes even to participate in intermediate-term trend reversals.
- No intraday action required.
- Works with many negatively and/or uncorrelated asset classes.
- Large per-trade profits when compared with shorter-term systems.

Disadvantages:

- Quicker response to intermediate-term reversals in these systems can result in oversensitivity to shorter-term fluctuation and a higher probability of being whipsawed than in the longer-term, lower-sensitivity systems.
  - To minimize intermediate-term whipsaws: Introduce a filter that sensitizes us to changes in volatility, such as ADX, following the trend of implied volatility of options.
- Positions require posting of overnight margin.

- Typically experiences poor win/loss ratios and a large number of consecutive losses.
- Still requires the ability to buy recent highs, sell recent lows, and relinquish a significant portion of unrealized profits.
- Smaller per-trade profits than longer-term trend-following systems.

Intermediate-term Mean Reversion with Trend-Following Filter

Typical duration of trade: 6 to 10 weeks
Examples: RSI extremes with moving average filter; Bollinger bands with moving average filter

Advantages:

- Because these systems capitalize on the market's propensity to revert to the mean, we can profit in either trending or choppy markets.
- Although they do entail more trading decisions than long-term trend-following systems, they are still relatively low maintenance/less psychologically stressful systems than the intraday decision-making process endured by day traders.
- These systems typically enjoy larger per-trade profits than day trading systems.
- These systems traditionally experience superior winning percentages and lower maximum consecutive losses than their trend-following counterparts.
- Because these systems capitalize on the market's propensity for mean reversion while simultaneously trading in the direction of the longer-term trend, they are often the easiest for traders to psychologically buy in to as a superior methodology.

    It is very appealing to simultaneously sell recent highs/buy recent lows while having the confidence inherent in trading in the direction of the longer-term trend. This ease of psychological acceptance suggests a higher probability of sticking with the system during its inevitable periods of equity drawdown.
- These systems sometimes initiate and/or exit trades with limit orders, thereby reducing slippage.
- Portfolio experiences flat periods: Because these systems rarely hold open positions in any particular market for significant durations, traders can benefit from the enhanced performance inherent in trading a portfolio of assets while simultaneously taking mental breaks from the stress of always holding open positions in the markets.

Disadvantages:

- Requires posting of overnight margins.
- Average size of losers is identical or sometimes even larger than the size of winners (and so it requires superior money management and iron-willed discipline).

    As stated earlier, fewer opportunities suggest the ability to exhibit unyielding patience and a willingness to watch from the sidelines until these rare opportunities unfold in the marketplace. A lack of discipline and patience often results in acceptance of inferior trading signals (e.g., taking trades with either a lower winning percentage or a poor profit/loss ratio).

- Small number of trade signals means diminished reliability of back-tested results (unless data sample is lengthened accordingly).
- Works consistently on only a limited number of diverse asset classes.

Short- to Intermediate-term Nondirectionally Biased Mean Reversion

Typical duration of trade: 3 to 8 weeks
Examples: Bollinger bands with ADX filter; slow stochastics with CCI filter; slow stochastics with CCI filter and time exit

Advantages:

- Because these systems have no directional bias, they generate a larger number of trading opportunities than systems with trend-following filters.
- Shorter duration of trades means more trading opportunities.
- Increased number of trades improves reliability of backtested results.
- Unlike many traditional trend-following strategies, these systems (like most mean reversion techniques) quantify both risk and reward prior to initiation of the trade. This results in exiting with profits via limit orders, which suggests lower per-trade slippage than trend trading.

Disadvantages:

- Elimination of the trend-following filter often results in less confidence in the trading system and higher probability of abandonment during drawdowns.
- More trading opportunities over a shorter time frame means more decisions and more stress.
- Works consistently on only a limited number of diverse asset classes.

Trend-Following Swing Trading

Typical duration of trade: 1 to 15 days

Example: Channel breakout with 15-day entry, 8-day exit, and 7.5-day time exit

Advantages:
- More opportunities over a shorter duration.
- Ability to profit from the shorter-term trending action unseen by longer-term players.
- Most strategies employ a time-driven exit criterion, which makes entry at recent highs or lows more psychologically palatable to many trend traders.
- Often employs a profit target exit with psychological benefits similar to those of the time-driven exits.

Disadvantages:
- Profitable on fewer assets—requires superior liquidity and volatility to compensate for endurance of identical, fixed transaction costs.
- Smaller per-trade profits.
- Exclusion of 24-hour traded asset classes for all except for institutional traders or trading teams.
- Intraday decisions means traders are married to the screen, which is much more stressful.

Mean Reversion Swing Trading with Trend-Following Filter

Typical duration of trade: 1 to 15 days
Example: RSI extremes with moving average filter

Advantages:
- Same benefits as enjoyed by intermediate-term traders, only now more signals are generated.
- Because the system generates more trading signals, vacations are easier.

Disadvantages:
- Works consistently on only a severely limited number of asset classes.
- Intraday decisions mean traders are married to the screen, which is much more stressful.
- Systems require more attention, refinement, and possible reevaluation than systems with longer time frames to ensure robustness. Because longer-term systems are tested over a longer duration and in multiple markets with low correlations, the backtested results are more robust (therefore requiring less refinement and/or possible reevaluation) than shorter-term systems.

Nondirectionally Biased Mean Reversion Swing Trading

Typical duration of trade: 1 to 15 days
Example: RSI crossover

Advantages:

- Same benefits as the intermediate-term traders, only now there are more signals generated.
- Because the system generates more trading signals, vacations are easier.
- Can capitalize on virtually any trading environment—trending, choppy, or mean reverting.

Disadvantages:

- Works consistently on only a severely limited number of asset classes.
- Intraday decisions means traders are married to the screen, which is much more stressful.
- Same as for "Mean Reversion Swing Trading with Trend-following Filter."

Mean Reversion Day Trading with Trend-Following Filter

Typical duration of trade: minutes to hours
Example: RSI extremes with moving average filter

Advantages:

- Employment of the trend-following filter enables participation in the short- to intermediate-term trend, while still being able to capitalize on intermediate- to longer-term sideways market behavior.
- Trading in the direction of the short- to intermediate-term trend leads to greater confidence when fading recent highs or lows.
- No overnight margins and ability to "clear your head" at close of each trading day.
- More trading opportunities.
- With proper money management, each trade should risk small percentage of working capital.
- Ability to implement with some degree of success on very short time frames.

Disadvantages:

- More decisions mean more stress.
- Smaller per-trade profits means few vehicles exhibit enough volatility and liquidity to be profitable.
- Must fight tendency to overtrade or risk losing discipline and/or consistency.

Nondirectionally Biased Mean Reversion Day Trading

Typical duration of trade: minutes to hours
Example: RSI crossover

Advantages:

- Can capitalize on virtually any trading environment—trending, choppy, or mean reverting.
- No overnight margins and ability to "clear one's head" at close of each trading day.
- More trading opportunities.
- With proper money management, each trade should risk small percentage of working capital.

Disadvantages:

- More decisions mean more stress.
- Smaller per-trade profits mean few vehicles are volatile and liquid enough to be profitable.
- Must fight tendency to overtrade or risk losing discipline and/or consistency.
- Off-floor disadvantage: loss of the bid/ask spread and/or higher commissions. Because such costs are fixed, as time frames are shortened, the viability of these strategies becomes marginalized.

CHAPTER 7

System Development and Analysis

Benefits and Pitfalls

*All truths are easy to understand once they are
discovered; the point is to discover them.*

—Galileo

SYSTEM DEVELOPMENT ISSUES: AN OVERVIEW

Mechanical trading systems offer traders a multitude of benefits, including quantification of risk, reward, and assessment of percentage of winning trades prior to entry, along with a host of others. However, for every benefit, there are pitfalls to be avoided and/or (in some instances) accepted as the price paid for enjoyment of such benefits.

The first and most obvious problem in the system development process is that all decisions made regarding trading systems are based on historical data. Future market behavior will never look exactly like the past, and because all models are based on extrapolations from historical data, the best we can hope for is a strong positive correlation between past and future market behavior.

Because decisions regarding indicators and parameter sets for our trading systems are determined through our study of historical data, the methods used to ensure the robustness of our systems must address this limitation in the system development process. Although this statement seems so obvious that it is almost not worth mentioning, the ramifications of this simple truth are far-reaching and underestimation of this flaw leads to a significant number of the errors commonly committed in the system development process.

BENEFITS OF MECHANICAL TRADING SYSTEMS

This section acts both as a comprehensive review of those benefits enjoyed by those employing mechanical trading systems and as an opportunity to examine other benefits not previously addressed.

The greatest benefit of mechanical trading systems is their ability to reprogram traders away from destructive types of behavior in favor of successful trading habits. Although this reprogramming process is typically a long and painstaking one, for those who have a single-minded desire to succeed (see Chapter 11), it is a powerful tool in tempering emotionalism as well as fostering discipline, patience, and adherence to principles of sound price risk management.

Another benefit enjoyed by those employing mechanical trading systems is quantification of risk and reward in general, along with the ability to quantify the risk/reward for an entire portfolio of assets. Without the quantification of risk and reward, performance forecasting is problematic. Moreover, although prudent price risk management is not dependent on utilization of a mechanical trading system per se, the ability to quickly compare historical results of a system to current performance and to determine whether these deviations are within normal tolerances or suggestive of a paradigm shift in market dynamics is invaluable to both traders and risk managers.

As stated earlier, because the mechanical trading systems showcased throughout this book are based on mathematical technical indicators, they require system developers to have significantly less specialized knowledge than other market participants regarding the underlying fundamentals affecting a particular market. Absence of this prerequisite expertise allows traders to apply their system or systems to trade various assets with negative and/or low correlations.

In addition, traders also can execute various transactions simultaneously in multiple systems exhibiting negative and/or low correlations, such as trend-following and intermediate-term mean reverting systems. Finally, because many mechanical system traders base entry and exit decisions on mathematical technical indicators, their performance typically will display a negative and/or low correlation to those of fundamental and/or discretionary technical traders.

PITFALLS OF MECHANICAL TRADING SYSTEMS

Data Integrity Issues Revisited

To understand the performance tables presented throughout Chapter 3, I discussed two specific data integrity issues: methods of accurately backtesting futures contracts (which accounted for contract expiration issues) and point value versus percentage changes in the data history. Here I merely reiterate their importance in maintenance of data integrity. If either of these issues is germane to readers' data history, please review that chapter.

The next data integrity issue that must be addressed is the accuracy of data. This issue is an absolute prerequisite for developing any meaningful conclusions regarding the success or failure of a particular trading system both now and in the future, and yet this problem is often neglected and/or assumed away.

For most high-end data vendors covering exchange-traded instruments, the problem commonly known as bad ticks has steadily improved over the years in terms of both severity of occurrences and speed at which these erroneous data prints are fixed. Because the ability of each data vendor to handle these issues varies over time, I want to reiterate that accuracy in this area is an unyielding prerequisite for system developers, and it is the one aspect of system development in which superior quality must override any and all cost concerns.

The other issue regarding bad data pertains to non–exchange-traded instruments. It is no accident that with the exception of the extraordinarily transparent and liquid cash foreign exchange market, all the assets highlighted throughout this book trade on a major exchange. Except for cash treasuries and foreign exchange markets, at the time of this book's publication, whenever we leave realm of exchange-traded instruments, data integrity diminishes dramatically.

Aside from the lack of transparency of non–exchange-traded instruments, the other reason I avoid discussing them is their lack of liquidity. It is worth repeating that underestimation of slippage due to inferior liquidity can have a dramatic impact on the integrity of our backtested system results. Moreover, these effects are magnified as trading time frames are shortened (as exemplified in Table 5.1).

For professional money managers and others marketing hypothetically backtested results to the investment world, I always advise overestimation of slippage and commissions effects on hypothetical performance results. Investors tend to expect future performance to look like past performance. Because this is rarely the case, we must decide whether we want our real-time rate of return to worst drawdown ratios to outperform or underperform hypothetically backtested results. If an institutional investor allocates $5 million based on an expectation that drawdowns will not exceed 12 percent, the ability to weather a real-time drawdown of 20 percent is probably slim. By contrast, I have yet to hear of a trader losing institutional investment capital due to better than expected real-time profit to maximum drawdown ratios.

Finally, data integrity issues must account for realistic entry and exit price levels. Many of these issues were addressed in Chapters 3 and 4. Chapter 3 discussed why use of the following day's opening price on conditionally triggered intermediate- or long-term trading signals was preferable to that of either closing or intraday prices. Chapter 4 argued in favor of assuming losses instead of profits when trading systems achieved profit targets and stop loss levels on the same day.

Other realistic entry and exit levels issues include accounting for gaps beyond "theoretical" fill prices and filtering out trade executions (also known as fills) at opening price levels during a trading day in which futures contracts remain "locked limit." (Locked limit is a day in which no trading occurs due to a price shock event such as a surprising government report released after trading hours or overnight occurrence of a natural disaster.)[1]

Data Integrity: Considerations with Backtested Portfolio Results

Another data integrity issue examined earlier was limitations inherent in backtested portfolio results for long- to intermediate-term trading systems. To reiterate, the problem in analysis of a portfolio of assets (as opposed to a single instrument) is that there is no way of determining the portfolio's real-time worst peak-to-valley drawdown. As a result, system developers will instead look at the worst peak-to-valley drawdown for long- or intermediate-term portfolios based on trade exit dates.

By definition, such sacrifices of data integrity compromise the accuracy of this most essential measure of performance. Nevertheless, if forced to choose between a moderate degree of uncertainty or fuzziness in estimation of drawdowns for a diversified portfolio of assets or absolute accuracy on a single asset, system developers almost universally embrace portfolio fuzziness as the lesser of these two evils.

The reason for system developers' preference for a backtested portfolio of diversified assets is simple: Backtested results on a single asset can be very misleading, suggesting a losing system where results on a diversified portfolio would show a viable one or, worse still, suggesting viability when a system should be discarded as unprofitable. (For other benefits, see Chapter 9.)

Backtested Data Series: Quantity, Quality, and Out of Sample

There are no absolute answers as to how much historical data is sufficient to ensure the robustness of backtested results. Instead there are only prudent rules of thumb, such as ensuring that our backtested environments include all the various types of market environments imaginable: bullish, bearish, sideways and trending.

The other factor instrumental in determining how much data will be sufficient is the typical duration of the system's trades. The longer the duration, the more data required to ensure a statistically significant sampling. This is why I included 10 years of data history for the long- to intermediate-term trading systems but only 7 months of history for our 5-minute trading system.

Data history for the long- to intermediate-term trading systems in Chapters 3 and 4 ran from December 31, 1992, to December 31, 2002. I set aside the year 2003 for use in this chapter to ensure that these systems continue to work with the most recent data sampling available. (This practice is known as *walk-forward* or out-of-sample testing. If done correctly, it increases the probability of a high correlation between backtested performance results and those experienced in real-time trading accounts.) Why did I decide to use 10 years of backtesting on long- to intermediate-term systems with one year (2003) as my out-of-sample data history? Although I could have chosen to go back farther (e.g., 20 years), the farther we go back in time, the less our data will tend to reflect current market dynamics.

A comparison of the performance results from 1993 to 2002 (see Figure 7.1) of the channel breakout system for spot British pound–U.S. dollar versus the results generated from 1983 to 2002 in Figure 7.2 emphatically illustrates the point that more is not always better. Of course the data from 1983 to 1992 should be considered valid; but should it be given the same weighting as last year's data? Probably not.

Perhaps a viable alternative is retention of the longer-term data with the introduction of an exponential or linear weighting factor. This solution enables retention of the larger data sampling while simultaneously giving greater weight to the most recent data history. Obviously employment of such a solution raises its own problems, namely how much weighting on the most recent data is too much and how much is too little. Unfortunately, as with the question of the length of the data series itself, there are no absolute answers. Instead, readers are encouraged to experiment with various weighting factors on a case-by-case basis until a reasonable and statistically significant solution is found.

System Integrity: Avoiding the Pitfalls

As stated at the beginning of this chapter, because the future will never look exactly the same as the past, our goal as system developers is to generate real-time performance results that display as high a positive correlation to backtested data as possible. We already have seen how assurance

O=	18237
H=	18496
L=	18177
L=	18442
Δ=	+208

30 Dec 02	
O=	16033
H=	16058
L=	16014
C=	16025

TotalNetProfit	=	-35630	MaximumWin	=	10630	MaxConsecLosses=	8
ClosedNetProfit=		-36650	AverageLoss	=	-2363	CurConsecLosses=	5
TotalTradeCount=		79	MaximumLoss	=	-7190	ProfitToMaxDraw=	-0.61
OpenPosition	=	100000	MaxClosedDraw	=	-17160	ProfitLossRatio=	0.69
PercentLong	=	51	MaxDrawAmount	=	-58320	PercentWinners	=	37.97
AverageDuration=		34	MaxDrawDuration=		2520	RemoveToNeutral=	0.00
AverageProfit	=	-451	MaxConsecWins	=	5	TimePercentage	=	99.38
AverageWin	=	2673	CurConsecWins	=	0	CurDrawDown	=	-43340

FIGURE 7.1 Spot British pound/U.S. dollar with 20-day channel breakout. Includes data from December 30, 1992, to December 30, 2002.

Note: All trade summaries include $100 round-turn trade deductions for slippage and commissions. ©2004 CQG, Inc. All rights reserved worldwide.

O=	18113
H=	18140
L=	17910
L=	18030^
Δ=	-87

31 Dec 02	
O=	16018
H=	16133
L=	16009
C=	16096

TotalNetProfit	=	171750	MaximumWin	=	34870	MaxConsecLosses=	8
ClosedNetProfit=		170020	AverageLoss	=	-2794	CurConsecLosses=	5
TotalTradeCount=		138	MaximumLoss	=	-9770	ProfitToMaxDraw=	2.51
OpenPosition	=	100000	MaxClosedDraw	=	-19500	ProfitLossRatio=	1.83
PercentLong	=	50	MaxDrawAmount	=	-68480	PercentWinners	=	46.38
AverageDuration=		39	MaxDrawDuration=		2630	RemoveToNeutral=	5.84
AverageProfit	=	1245	MaxConsecWins	=	7	TimePercentage	=	99.90
AverageWin	=	5914	CurConsecWins	=	0	CurDrawDown	=	-52790

FIGURE 7.2 Spot British pound/U.S. dollar with 20-day channel breakout. Includes data from December 31, 1982, to December 31, 2002.

Note: All trade summaries include $100 round-turn trade deductions for slippage and commissions. ©2004 CQG, Inc. All rights reserved worldwide.

of data integrity aids in attainment of this goal. Next we examine how the integrity of the trading system itself can ensure the highest possible correlations between our historical and future performance.

Checking the System's Integrity

The ability of computers to generate and backtest various concepts quickly and efficiently has been one of the great leaps forward for traders and system developers. Because we can now determine profitability, win/loss ratios, and profit to maximum drawdown with such ease, it is tempting simply to tinker through the virtually limitless permutations of trading parameters until we find those that best resonate with our trading personality types. This "tinkering" process satisfies both the scientist and the trader in us, and our ability to generate backtested performance results with such speed and efficiency often lulls us into a false sense of security regarding accuracy. Consequently, I remind readers that generated performance results are only as accurate as the ability of programming code to capture desired entry and exit conditions.

The only way to avoid the problem of faulty programming code and to ensure the integrity of a trading system's performance results is the painstaking and tedious process known as *spot checking*. Spot checking entails running through the entire trade list results for the system and comparing these against the full data history. Even prior to combing through the details of the entire data history, a quick review of the performance summary tables often can clue us in to programming flaws. Examples of these anomalies in performance tables include 0 or 100 percent of trading signals generated being long positions, average length of trades being atypically short or long in duration or 0 or 100 percent of trades being losses.

Once the scan of performance tables has been completed, the spot-checking process should commence. Here we should seek answers to these questions:

- Were conditions for entry and exit met?
- Were trades initiated?
- Was it at the intended price level?
- Were commissions and/or slippage deducted from profits and added to losses?[2]

As with the data integrity issues, until indisputably satisfactory answers to these spot-checking questions are attained, continuation of trading system analysis is pointless.

An entirely different aspect of system checking is the process that Robert Pardo, pioneering author of the book on trading system development, calls *theory checking*. Theory checking examines the performance of the system in terms of how the actual backtested results conformed to theoretical expectations. Divergence between expectations and actual results is not necessarily a fatal flaw in theory checking, as it is in spot checking, so long as the generated results are still attractive in terms of viability of the system and its compatibility to our own particular trading temperaments.

The main questions the theory checking process seeks to answer are: Did the system perform as intended? Did it profit in trending or choppy markets? Were the average trade duration, win/loss ratio, and profit to maximum drawdown ratios experienced similar to initial assumptions? And, if not, why did they differ from these expectations?[3] Personally, I have always felt that the primary point in theory checking is to determine whether initial assumptions regarding the trading system in question were erroneous or if the particular data series examined was in some manner atypical.

OPTIMIZATION PROCESS

An Overview

Optimization is the process of tweaking the raw trading system by adjusting its parameters (or variables—e.g., number of days, indicator-driven triggers such as moving averages, price-driven triggers such as channel breakout, etc.) and/or parameter sets (or combination of parameter values—e.g., a two moving average crossover system utilizing 9- and 26-day moving averages).[4] Optimization is a valuable aspect of the system development process because, without this essential step, we would be forced simply to accept whatever performance results were generated by our system's default parameters and parameter sets. Without optimization we might falsely believe a successful system to be unprofitable or, worse still, that a losing system is profitable.

Despite these undeniable benefits, optimization is not without its drawbacks. Modification of parameters and/or parameters sets can easily lead to false expectations regarding the future performance of a system. As with most tools, optimization has its utility, but this utility can be actualized only if the process is employed with diligence toward the scientific process and an awareness of its inherent limitations.

Optimization: Benefits

In addition to the benefits just outlined, optimization enables system developers to test out broad theoretical concepts regarding market behavior (e.g., the market's propensity to trend, to revert to the mean following a parabolic directional move, etc.) prior to commitment of real money. Even if we are fairly confident in the robustness of a particular theory regarding market behavior, such confidence is a far cry from estimations of profit to maximum drawdown ratios, win/loss ratios, and the like.

Another key benefit to optimization studies is their ability to provide a historical benchmark of system performance that can then be used to compare against real-time trading results. Because the dynamics of markets are constantly changing, this ability to measure performance against the past can quickly clue us in to paradigm shifts requiring our revision and/or abandonment of trading systems.[5]

Optimization also shows us a trading system's entire spectrum of expected performance results (over a wide variety of parameter sets) prior to the commitment of capital; this increases our odds of determining the best set of values for our particular personality traits in terms of average duration of trade, maximum consecutive losses, and win/loss ratio. Psychological trader profiles have been discussed at length already; here I simply reiterate that traders' definitions of optimal performance results differ based on their own personalities. The optimization process helps them to avoid an incompatible system and/or parameter set.[6]

Finally optimization is an invaluable tool in the identification and avoidance of suboptimal parameter sets. In his book *Schwager on Futures: Technical Analysis*, Jack Schwager convincingly demonstrates a disturbingly low correlation between historically optimal parameter sets and the optimal parameters sets uncovered through the walk-forward (or out-of-sample) process. Despite such limitations, Schwager notes that one redeeming aspect of the optimization process is that it consistently identifies suboptimal parameter sets, and that such parameter sets remain suboptimal throughout the out-of-sample testing process.[7]

Limited Utility of Optimization Studies

As of this writing, data vendors cannot optimize entire portfolios of assets. Consequently, the best parameter set for each asset is not likely to be same as the best parameter set for a diversified portfolio. Furthermore, even if data vendors offering backtesting and optimization studies could determine the best parameter set for a diversified portfolio on any particular system, this parameter set probably would not retain its status as top performer if it were simultaneously traded in conjunction with another low- and/or negatively correlated system (e.g., trend-following and mean reversion systems).

Optimization: Avoiding the Pitfalls

The most obvious pitfall in system development in general, and in the optimization process specifically, is known as *curve fitting*. Curve fitting can be broken down into two basic subcategories: data curve fitting and parameter curve fitting. Data curve fitting occurs when system developers eliminate a portion of their historical data or intentionally reduce their historical data series at the study's outset to filter out losing trades.

Avoidance of data curve fitting in the system development process can be achieved through strict adherence to an objective data history criterion for backtesting of the trading system. As stated earlier, such data histories should include all types of market environments: bullish, bearish, trending, and mean reverting. If data histories do not contain all types of market environments, either we need to expand the data set to include more history or, if there is a lack of history for a particular trading vehicle, we should examine an asset that displays a strong positive correlation to the asset that we anticipate trading and whose history does include all types of market environments.

Parameter curve fitting can be defined as the practice of the system developer adapting trade criteria parameters to match or fit in-sample data. For example, let us return to the simple and robust moving average crossover system examined in Chapter 3. Because this system contained only two parameters (9- and 26-day moving averages), we were moderately confident that its future performance would display a strong positive correlation to its backtested data history. But suppose that system developers were dissatisfied with the poor win/loss ratio of the two moving average crossovers. They decide to search through a list of various indicators until discovering one that improves the win/loss ratio without negatively impacting other performance measures. Two things have now occurred: (1) the system gets fewer trading signals, and (2) the desired result is achieved—the remaining signals generate more winning trades than losers. Then the developers reason that if the addition of one new parameter made the system more successful, imagine what two, three or four more could do.

Eventually the addition of parameters results in the developers sacrificing a very robust and moderately successful trading system in favor of one that works perfectly in the past and terribly in the future. Remember, the more parameters added to a trading system, the more closely that system's criteria has been fit to the data. The closer the parameters have been fit to a particular data history, the less likely that these criteria will be able to filter out randomness within the data series.[8]

The easiest method to eliminate parameter curve fitting is to test and trade a system containing only one parameter. Unfortunately, although such a system would be the most robust imaginable, the likelihood of a one-parameter trading system being profitable is slim. Therefore, system developers must seek to balance the need for the fewest parameters possible in their systems while still maintaining optimal performance.

Aside from the establishment of an objective limit to the number of parameters that any particular trading system can contain, various methods can be employed to prevent parameter curve fitting. Such methods include backtesting of the system on a diversified portfolio of assets over a statistically significant data series (e.g., the portfolio employed in Chapter 3 over 10 years), along with the utilization of an out-of-sample data series.

Both data and parameter curve fitting are the result of a psychological trading problem that I have termed the *perfect trader syndrome*. The motivation is a combination of the need to be perfect and a desire to eliminate uncertainty and gain control over an uncertain future. Often the perfect trader syndrome leads us to seek the holy grail of trading and spend thousands of dollars on bogus systems promising winning trading percentages in excess of 90 percent. Remember, our goal in trading is not perfection; it is simply to manage risk well enough to enable us to consistently employ a trading methodology that will be successful over the long-term.

In his book, *Design, Testing and Optimization of Trading Systems*, Robert Pardo discusses a phenomenon that he calls *outlier curve fitting*. Outlier curve fitting occurs when a single trade makes up a disproportionate percentage of a trading system's profits (Pardo specifically warns against performance histories in which a single trade accounts for over 30 percent of a system's profits.[9]) Certain types of trading systems are more susceptible to this problem than others. In general, because mean reversion trading systems exit with profits when the market reverts to its mean, outlier curve fitting is unlikely. By contrast, trend-following systems have a much greater tendency to contain single, disproportionately large profitable trades within their performance histories.

The problem of including such outliers within performance results is that a single trade could distort the system's results, thereby leading us to believe that a system is robust and profitable, when in fact its success is due entirely to a single price shock event (e.g., the 1987 stock market crash). In extreme cases, such as those in which a single profit accounts for over 30 percent of a system's profits, exclusion of the outlier is probably prudent. Although it is the simplest solution to this problem, in less extreme cases, exclusion probably is not the preferred response.

Elimination of outliers from the data series is usually justified with the myth that such occurrences are aberrations in market behavior and are unlikely to be repeated in the future. This belief in outliers as unrepeatable aberrations contradicts the whole premise behind trend trading, namely that trend-following systems enable participation in the amplified tails of the market's distribution (see the discussion of stable Paretian distributions in Chapter 1). Intimately linked with this concept of outliers as aberrations is the myth that trend traders have a 50-50 chance of being caught on either side of the outlier. In reality, because outlier events typically are preceded by some type of technical breakout in the direction of the event, the odds of trend trader participation on the profitable side of the outlier are significantly greater than the 50 percent myth would lead us to believe. By the same token, a major drawback to the utilization of nondirectionally biased mean reversion systems is their greater propensity to suffering losses due to outlier events.

Finally, a subtler problem entailed in the exclusion of outliers from data history is that once the event has been removed, its reintroduction for price risk management purposes such as stress testing of the system (see Chapter 8) is often difficult to justify.

The Mechanics of Optimization

Now that we have outlined both the benefits and pitfalls of optimization studies, we can proceed with an examination of the preferred mechanics to employ in attempt to ensure the greatest utility of our optimization studies. To reiterate, the primary goal in our optimization studies is not pinpoint accuracy in forecasting of future performance. Instead, it is merely identification of historically robust parameters and parameter sets in the hope that such trade system criteria will continue to display positive correlations to past performance.

To review, consistency and data integrity in our optimization studies are crucial prerequisites in obtaining meaningful conclusions. I define "consistency" as the application of the same rules regarding entry, exit, and transaction costs throughout the entire backtested data series. Regarding data integrity, ideally our backtested data series should cover a diversified portfolio of assets and include all types of market environments: bullish, bearish, trending, choppy, neutral, and volatile.

Once this preliminary groundwork has been firmly established, we need to determine criteria for our choice of parameters and parameter sets. In choosing trading system parameters, we are seeking those that display the greatest propensity of enabling our participation in general principles of market behavior (e.g., mean reversion and/or trending). Regarding our testing of particular parameter sets in our optimization studies, the key here is inclusion of a broad and diverse group of parameter sets. There are two reasons for this:

1. Broad and diversified parameter sets improve our odds of identifying a robust set that will have a high probability of future positive correlations to our backtested history.[10]
2. Perhaps more important, the broader and more diversified our parameter sets, the greater the probability of our identification and subsequent elimination of suboptimal parameter sets.[11]

Before examining the mechanics of optimization studies in detail, it is important to identify an objective measure of performance that will allow us to distinguish between more and less robust parameter sets and trading systems quickly and efficiently. Although readers are encouraged to experiment with the entire spectrum of performance measures, I feel that the profit to maximum drawdown ratio (P:MD) outlined is one of the most efficient tools for distinguishing between robust and suboptimal parameter sets and trading systems.

The process of choosing which parameter sets to trade almost always proves more difficult than that of eliminating suboptimal parameter sets. Why is deciding on a particular parameter set so tough? Because the top-performing parameter sets for one asset are rarely the top performers for other negatively and/or uncorrelated assets. Furthermore, top performers in the past are often the laggards of the future. These points are well illustrated by my optimization study on the two moving average crossover system for the same portfolio of assets in Chapter 3 (see Tables 7.1 to 7.20).

In my optimization study of the two moving average crossover system, I chose to examine shorter-term moving average values between 6 and 10 days using a one-step interval (i.e., 6, 7, 8, 9, and 10) and longer-term moving average values set between 20 and 32 days using three-step intervals (i.e., 20, 23, 26, 29, and 32). The reason behind choosing a particular set of values in an optimization study is a function of utility, distinctiveness, experience, and common sense.

For example, for shorter-term moving averages, there is quite a significant difference between a 6- and 7-day moving average (e.g., increases the data series by one-sixth). By contrast, for the longer-term moving average, use of one-step variations in our optimization study is probably not going to yield the same distinctiveness in our data series as will be achieved by staggering our steps by three. This is because the difference between a 31- and a 32-day moving average only increases the data series by $1/31^{st}$ and is therefore minute.[12]

In choosing which values to include and exclude from the study, I began with the exclusion of nonsensical values (e.g., 2 days as a value for our short-term moving average) and worked forward based on values used most commonly by technicians in the markets (e.g., 7 days for the shorter-term moving average and 29 days for the longer-term moving average). Although this method is far from infallible, the goal in an optimization study is not perfection, but merely the identification of diverse, robust parameter sets and avoidance of suboptimal sets.

In examining the tables, notice how rarely the top performer of the 10-year "in-sample" period was the top performer in our "out-of-sample" period. Perhaps even more disturbing is the significant number of times that our worst-performing parameter set during our "in-sample" period

TABLE 7.1 Moving average crossover optimization for NYBOT cotton
(1993–2002).

Short Moving Average	Long Moving Average	P:MD
7	*29*	*0.24*
6	26	−0.06
7	32	−0.09
8	29	−0.11
8	26	−0.12
9	29	−0.12
10	26	−0.16
10	23	−0.21
9	**26**	**−0.22**
6	29	−0.22
9	32	−0.25
10	29	−0.26
8	32	−0.26
9	23	−0.28
8	23	−0.30
6	32	−0.35
7	26	−0.37
7	23	−0.38
10	32	−0.39
10	20	−0.43
9	20	−0.49
8	20	−0.63
6	23	−0.66
6	20	−0.69
7	*20*	*−0.70*

Note: All trade summaries include $100 round-turn trade deductions for slippage
and commissions. Data source: CQG, Inc.

TABLE 7.2 Moving average crossover optimization for NYBOT cotton (2003).

Short Moving Average	Long Moving Average	P:MD
10	20	1.59
6	20	1.48
7	20	1.30
8	20	1.25
10	29	1.22
7	23	1.17
6	23	1.13
8	23	1.11
9	20	1.05
9	29	1.04
6	26	0.91
10	26	0.88
8	26	0.83
7	*29*	*0.83*
9	32	0.82
10	23	0.76
6	29	0.76
9	**26**	**0.72**
6	32	0.69
7	26	0.67
8	29	0.65
8	32	0.64
10	32	0.63
7	32	0.62
9	23	0.42

Note: All trade summaries include $100 round-turn trade deductions for slippage and commissions. Data source: CQG, Inc.

TABLE 7.3 Moving average crossover optimization for NYMEX crude oil (1993–2000).

Short Moving Average	Long Moving Average	P:MD
8	*26*	*1.64*
9	**26**	**1.34**
7	32	1.30
6	20	1.21
8	32	1.16
8	23	1.14
9	29	1.13
8	29	1.06
6	26	1.04
7	29	0.99
7	26	0.96
9	23	0.92
7	23	0.91
10	29	0.90
10	26	0.87
10	20	0.84
6	32	0.81
9	32	0.68
6	23	0.66
6	29	0.53
7	20	0.49
10	23	0.45
8	20	0.43
9	20	0.43
10	*32*	*0.39*

Note: All trade summaries include $100 round-turn trade deductions for slippage and commissions. Data source: CQG, Inc.

TABLE 7.4 Moving average crossover optimization for NYMEX crude oil—out-of-sample study (2003).

Short Moving Average	Long Moving Average	P:MD
6	32	0.14
6	29	−0.02
7	32	−0.13
7	29	−0.34
9	29	−0.34
10	29	−0.34
8	32	−0.37
7	26	−0.39
8	29	−0.42
6	26	−0.45
10	*32*	*−0.52*
9	20	−0.54
9	32	−0.54
7	23	−0.59
10	26	−0.60
9	**26**	**−0.65**
8	*26*	*−0.66*
10	23	−0.67
6	23	−0.68
10	20	−0.71
8	23	−0.71
8	20	−0.74
7	20	−0.75
9	23	−0.75
6	20	−0.76

Note: All trade summaries include $100 round-turn trade deductions for slippage and commissions. Data source: CQG, Inc.

TABLE 7.5 Moving average crossover optimization for CBOT T-notes (1993–2002).

Short Moving Average	Long Moving Average	P:MD
10	*23*	*2.28*
9	29	2.28
10	29	2.18
8	26	2.03
10	26	2.02
9	**26**	**1.63**
8	29	1.50
9	32	1.48
10	32	1.47
7	26	1.32
8	32	1.30
7	32	1.15
9	23	1.06
8	23	0.64
7	29	0.61
6	26	0.58
7	23	0.56
10	20	0.30
6	23	0.21
8	20	0.12
6	32	−0.03
6	29	−0.10
6	20	−0.30
9	20	−0.30
7	*20*	*−0.45*

Note: All trade summaries include $100 round-turn trade deductions for slippage and commissions. Data source: CQG, Inc.

TABLE 7.6 Moving average crossover optimization for CBOT T-notes—out-of-sample study (2003).

Short Moving Average	Long Moving Average	P:MD
6	26	0.60
6	23	0.34
7	23	0.27
10	26	0.16
9	20	0.15
6	20	0.13
7	26	0.13
10	32	0.13
9	**26**	**0.12**
8	32	0.11
9	32	0.11
6	29	0.09
7	*20*	*0.08*
10	29	0.08
10	*23*	*0.07*
8	26	0.07
9	29	0.07
8	29	0.05
8	23	0.04
9	23	0.01
7	29	0.00
10	20	−0.03
7	32	−0.04
6	32	−0.10
8	20	−0.30

Note: All trade summaries include $100 round-turn trade deductions for slippage and commissions. Data source: CQG, Inc.

TABLE 7.7 Moving average crossover optimization for COMEX gold
(1993–2002).

Short Moving Average	Long Moving Average	P:MD
10	*29*	*0.08*
10	32	−0.07
10	26	−0.22
7	32	−0.40
9	32	−0.40
10	23	−0.41
9	**26**	**−0.43**
6	32	−0.43
7	29	−0.46
9	23	−0.49
9	29	−0.49
8	29	−0.51
10	20	−0.53
8	32	−0.54
8	26	−0.64
6	29	−0.64
8	23	−0.68
9	20	−0.69
7	23	−0.72
7	26	−0.74
6	23	−0.77
8	20	−0.78
6	26	−0.78
6	20	−0.81
7	*20*	*−0.81*

Note: All trade summaries include $100 round-turn trade deductions for slippage
and commissions. Data source: CQG, Inc.

TABLE 7.8 Moving average crossover optimization for COMEX gold—out-of-sample study (2003).

Short Moving Average	Long Moving Average	P:MD
10	*29*	*1.90*
8	26	1.80
9	**26**	**1.80**
10	26	1.71
7	29	1.62
9	29	1.40
9	32	1.36
8	29	1.30
9	23	1.29
10	23	1.27
8	32	1.23
7	32	1.22
10	20	1.19
7	23	1.12
8	23	1.00
10	32	1.00
6	29	0.99
6	23	0.95
9	20	0.93
7	26	0.93
6	32	0.90
6	26	0.72
8	20	0.55
7	*20*	*0.45*
6	20	0.39

Note: All trade summaries include $100 round-turn trade deductions for slippage and commissions. Data source: CQG, Inc.

TABLE 7.9 Moving average crossover optimization for CBOT soybeans (1993–2002).

Short Moving Average	Long Moving Average	P:MD
10	*26*	*0.70*
9	29	0.58
8	29	0.39
7	26	0.34
8	26	0.31
9	32	0.24
7	29	0.18
9	**26**	**0.17**
10	29	0.16
10	32	0.08
8	32	−0.12
8	23	−0.13
7	23	−0.20
6	26	−0.22
6	23	−0.27
7	32	−0.30
9	23	−0.35
10	23	−0.36
8	20	−0.38
6	29	−0.41
6	32	−0.45
6	20	−0.51
10	20	−0.62
9	20	−0.72
7	*20*	*−0.79*

Note: All trade summaries include $100 round-turn trade deductions for slippage and commissions. Data source: CQG, Inc.

TABLE 7.10 Moving average crossover optimization for CBOT soybeans—out-of-sample study (2003).

Short Moving Average	Long Moving Average	P:MD
10	20	1.94
6	23	1.13
7	*20*	*1.07*
6	20	0.93
10	32	0.92
7	23	0.89
9	20	0.83
10	29	0.77
8	20	0.74
10	*26*	*0.73*
6	26	0.53
8	23	0.51
10	23	0.22
9	23	0.16
6	32	−0.01
8	29	−0.08
9	29	−0.10
7	32	−0.11
9	32	−0.11
6	29	−0.14
8	32	−0.16
8	26	−0.24
7	26	−0.29
7	29	−0.38
9	**26**	**−0.39**

Note: All trade summaries include $100 round-turn trade deductions for slippage and commissions. Data source: CQG, Inc.

TABLE 7.11 Moving average crossover optimization for CME lean hogs
(1993–2002).

Short Moving Average	Long Moving Average	P:MD
10	*26*	*1.52*
9	**26**	**1.38**
8	32	0.81
9	23	1.52
8	29	0.80
8	26	1.04
7	29	0.79
7	32	0.68
10	23	1.04
9	20	0.96
9	32	0.59
9	29	0.55
6	32	0.57
10	20	0.82
10	29	0.57
10	32	0.36
6	29	0.40
7	26	0.29
8	23	0.18
6	26	0.15
6	23	0.17
7	23	0.03
8	20	−0.26
7	20	−0.25
6	20	−0.42

Note: All trade summaries include $100 round-turn trade deductions for slippage
and commissions. Data source: CQG, Inc.

TABLE 7.12 Moving average crossover optimization for CME lean hogs—out-of-sample study (2003).

Short Moving Average	Long Moving Average	P:MD
6	32	0.86
9	23	0.58
7	32	0.48
8	23	0.38
9	20	0.34
10	20	0.34
9	**26**	**0.25**
10	23	0.23
7	20	0.21
7	29	0.19
8	26	0.18
7	23	0.13
6	20	0.06
8	20	0.05
6	29	0.05
9	29	0.03
8	29	0.02
10	*26*	*−0.06*
7	26	−0.07
6	26	−0.10
10	32	−0.12
10	29	−0.13
6	23	−0.19
8	32	−0.21
9	32	−0.21

Note: All trade summaries include $100 round-turn trade deductions for slippage and commissions. Data source: CQG, Inc.

TABLE 7.13 Moving average crossover optimization for CME eurodollars (1993–2002).

Short Moving Average	Long Moving Average	P:MD
7	*29*	*2.28*
8	32	2.20
9	32	2.18
9	29	2.17
6	29	2.11
9	23	2.06
7	32	1.96
10	29	1.72
8	29	1.71
10	32	1.71
9	20	1.53
10	23	1.51
8	23	1.49
8	20	1.30
8	26	1.26
10	26	1.26
10	20	1.17
6	32	1.14
7	26	1.04
9	**26**	**1.02**
7	20	0.95
7	23	0.72
6	20	0.69
6	26	0.59
6	*23*	*0.51*

Note: All trade summaries include $100 round-turn trade deductions for slippage and commissions. Data source: CQG, Inc.

TABLE 7.14 Moving average crossover optimization for CME eurodollars—out-of-sample study (2003).

Short Moving Average	Long Moving Average	P:MD
6	32	−0.91
6	20	−0.92
6	*23*	*−0.92*
7	20	−0.93
8	32	−0.94
9	32	−0.94
10	32	−0.94
6	29	−0.95
10	29	−0.95
7	32	−0.95
6	26	−0.96
7	*29*	*−0.96*
8	29	−0.96
9	29	−0.96
8	26	−0.97
9	**26**	**−0.97**
10	23	−0.97
7	26	−0.97
9	23	−0.97
8	23	−0.97
7	23	−0.97
10	26	−0.97
8	20	−0.98
9	20	−0.98
10	20	−0.98

Note: All trade summaries include $100 round-turn trade deductions for slippage and commissions. Data source: CQG, Inc.

TABLE 7.15 Moving average crossover optimization for CME Japanese yen (1993–2002).

Short Moving Average	Long Moving Average	P:MD
8	*29*	*5.16*
7	29	4.93
7	32	3.45
8	32	3.42
9	29	3.23
6	23	3.20
9	32	3.12
6	29	2.84
10	29	2.61
7	26	2.48
10	23	2.47
8	26	2.39
10	32	2.27
8	20	1.92
6	32	1.89
10	20	1.82
9	**26**	**1.81**
6	26	1.80
7	23	1.70
9	20	1.69
9	23	1.69
10	26	1.47
8	23	1.40
7	20	1.37
6	*20*	*1.13*

Note: All trade summaries include $100 round-turn trade deductions for slippage and commissions. Data source: CQG, Inc.

TABLE 7.16 Moving average crossover optimization for CME Japanese yen—out-of-sample study (2003).

Short Moving Average	Long Moving Average	P:MD
10	32	0.03
10	29	0.01
9	29	−0.06
6	23	−0.09
9	32	−0.18
9	23	−0.25
10	23	−0.25
8	26	−0.30
8	32	−0.33
7	23	−0.34
6	*20*	*−0.35*
10	20	−0.35
7	29	−0.35
7	26	−0.37
8	*29*	*−0.38*
10	26	−0.41
7	32	−0.41
8	23	−0.43
9	**26**	**−0.46**
6	26	−0.49
6	32	−0.58
7	20	−0.59
9	20	−0.59
8	20	−0.63
6	29	−0.66

Note: All trade summaries include $100 round-turn trade deductions for slippage and commissions. Data source: CQG, Inc.

TABLE 7.17 Moving average crossover optimization for CME Swiss franc (1993–2002).

Short Moving Average	Long Moving Average	P:MD
10	*29*	*1.76*
9	29	1.44
8	32	1.41
9	32	1.39
10	32	1.30
10	26	1.10
8	29	1.07
8	26	0.91
9	**26**	**0.72**
9	23	0.56
6	26	0.48
7	26	0.44
7	29	0.35
10	20	0.25
8	23	−0.11
9	20	−0.15
10	23	−0.18
8	20	−0.19
7	32	−0.19
6	23	−0.24
6	29	−0.24
7	23	−0.36
6	32	−0.45
7	20	−0.73
6	*20*	*−0.83*

Note: All trade summaries include $100 round-turn trade deductions for slippage and commissions. Data source: CQG, Inc.

TABLE 7.18 Moving average crossover optimization for CME Swiss franc—out-of-sample study (2003).

Short Moving Average	Long Moving Average	P:MD
7	20	0.83
6	26	0.77
10	23	0.71
7	32	0.70
6	23	0.63
8	32	0.58
7	26	0.55
7	23	0.54
8	23	0.50
6	32	0.47
10	32	0.46
9	20	0.45
8	29	0.40
10	20	0.36
9	32	0.36
6	*20*	*0.28*
8	20	0.26
7	29	0.24
9	23	0.20
8	26	0.16
10	26	0.16
6	29	0.11
9	**26**	**−0.02**
9	29	−0.13
10	*29*	***−0.36***

Note: All trade summaries include $100 round-turn trade deductions for slippage and commissions. Data source: CQG, Inc.

TABLE 7.19 Moving average crossover optimization for CME E-mini S&P 500 (1993–2002).

Short Moving Average	Long Moving Average	P:MD
10	*23*	*0.39*
8	20	0.27
7	20	0.24
10	20	0.02
9	20	−0.02
9	**26**	**−0.06**
10	26	−0.10
6	20	−0.11
9	23	−0.14
8	23	−0.16
7	23	−0.20
10	32	−0.25
8	26	−0.26
8	32	−0.27
9	32	−0.28
7	29	−0.29
6	26	−0.36
6	29	−0.37
8	29	−0.37
10	29	−0.44
9	29	−0.45
7	32	−0.50
6	23	−0.51
7	26	−0.53
6	*32*	*−0.59*

Note: All trade summaries include $100 round-turn trade deductions for slippage and commissions. Data source: CQG, Inc.

TABLE 7.20 Moving average crossover optimization for CME E-mini S&P 500—
out-of-sample study (2003).

Short Moving Average	Long Moving Average	P:MD
6	*32*	*0.83*
6	29	0.33
7	26	0.09
9	29	0.02
6	23	−0.06
8	32	−0.07
7	23	−0.10
10	29	−0.10
10	32	−0.10
7	32	−0.14
7	20	−0.15
9	32	−0.16
7	29	−0.17
6	26	−0.19
9	23	−0.31
8	23	−0.34
6	20	−0.35
10	26	−0.37
9	**26**	**−0.41**
8	29	−0.41
8	26	−0.46
10	*23*	*−0.47*
8	20	−0.48
9	20	−0.73
10	20	−0.76

Note: All trade summaries include $100 round-turn trade deductions for slippage
and commissions. Data source: CQG, Inc.

outperformed our top performer during the "out-of-sample" or walk-forward period.

If deciding on the superiority of a particular parameter set is often problematic, what can we conclude from our optimization studies on the two-moving average crossover system? Performance's dramatic variance from asset to asset and from year to year strengthens the argument in favor of diversification among a wide variety of parameter sets.[13] If choosing between a wide variety of robust parameter sets is such a frustrating task, then staggering entry and exit orders through all of the "acceptable" parameter sets seems like an attractive and rational alternative (assuming, of course, that such diversification among parameter sets does not result in abandonment of stringent principles of price risk management as outlined in Chapter 8).

Now that this study of the optimization results on the two moving average crossover system has shattered the myth of a single optimal parameter set, we can proceed to examine some basic principles of optimization. Despite the fact that there is no single optimal parameter set, there is nothing wrong with conducting an optimization study and then using it to identify various robust and distinct parameter sets. In analyzing such results, we seek to accomplish two goals: the elimination of suboptimal and nonsensical parameter sets (e.g., setting our shorter-term moving average to 2 days), and use of these results to identify various robust and distinct parameter sets.

The phenomenon known as profit spikes often makes the elimination of suboptimal parameter sets more difficult. Profit spikes are profitable parameter sets surrounded by those exhibiting consistently inferior performance. Pardo provides a sound mechanism to weed out such anomalies by averaging of profit spike parameter sets with those of neighboring parameter sets. This averaging technique helps both in eliminating aberrant performers that display a high probability of yielding suboptimal results going forward and in identifying more robust "hilltops" in performance. Such performance hilltops are superior performers that are adjacent to other similarly robust parameter sets.[14]

SYSTEM DEVELOPMENT PROCESS

Out-of-Sample Study

The out-of-sample or walk-forward study is probably one of the most important aspects of the system development process. This procedure of setting aside a statistically significant (and most up-to-date[15]) portion of the data series to ensure that the system is behaving as forecasted is crucial to system developers because it enables us to test the system prior to committing actual funds.

The most essential aspect of the out-of-sample data window is its integrity. Data integrity is defined here as the inability of our in-sample results to bleed through into our out-of-sample data. Although data integrity of the out-of-sample window might appear to be a given prerequisite, it never hurts to restate the obvious, especially since failure to adhere to this rule will necessarily compromise the value of all out-of-sample testing. Other, less critical characteristics of the out-of-ample window are that it generally should contain somewhere between 10 to 20 percent of the data displayed within the in-sample window.[16]

Although out-of-sample results never look exactly like those of our in-sample performance, there should be a strong positive correlation between the two data sets. If walk-forward performance yields results that are drastically different from those of in-sample data (e.g., postoptimization drawdowns exceeding 15 percent of in-sample), we probably should abandon the trading system. This seemingly drastic response to excessive drawdowns is prudent due to the nature of the optimization process.

Remember that the optimization process is one in which underperforming parameter sets are rejected in favor of robust ones. This process of filtering out poor performers can lead to an underestimation of the true risk entailed in employment of a particular trading system. There are only two ways to discover poor real-time performance of a trading system: the out-of-sample study and a real-time trading account. Consequently, the 15 percent rule seems a prudent alternative to the real-time failure of the trading system.[17]

Failure of the out-of-sample study is most commonly due either to data curve fitting (e.g., in-sample study was conducted on too few markets or too small of a data sample and as a result did not capture all types of market environments) or to parameter curve fitting.[18] Other possibilities could be an unprecedented shift in market dynamics. Such a shift is exemplified by the unprecedented increase in volatility exhibited by the Nymex natural gas contract (see Figure 7.3).

For example, if the in-sample study included Nymex natural gas data from 1990 to 1999 and the out-of-sample study included the same contract's data from the year 2000, there is a high probability that trading systems attempting to profit by fading unsustainable levels of volatility would have succeeded during our in-sample study and failed miserably in the out-of-sample study.

Traders and system developers alike must be ever mindful of paradigm shifts in market dynamics. Because markets are rarely stagnant, what worked in the past may not be robust enough to survive dramatic shifts in the dynamics of market behavior as exemplified by our study of natural gas in 2000. Despite our diligence in backtesting and forward (out-of-sample) testing of a wide variety of asset classes and market

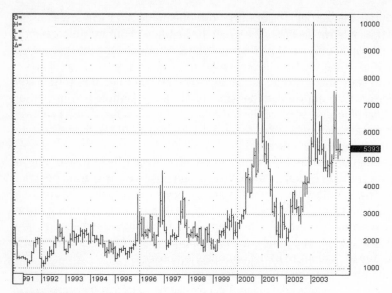

FIGURE 7.3   Rolling front-month Nymex natural gas futures.

Note: All trade summaries include $100 round-turn trade deductions for slippage and commissions. ©2004 CQG, Inc. All rights reserved worldwide.

environments, sometimes unprecedented shifts in market dynamics are too dramatic to enable utilization of previously successful trading systems (examples of such shifts occurred in agricultural markets in the 1970s and in metals markets in 1979 to 1980). In such instances, those who can quickly identify the paradigm shift in market behavior and make the necessary adjustments will outperform the remainder of the pack. This is why the ability to analyze the historical performance of trading systems is invaluable in distinguishing between an equity drawdown within "normal" system tolerances and a long-term and/or permanent paradigm shift in market behavior.

Limitations to the System Development and Data Analysis Process

I have already alluded to the fact that our ideals in terms of performance results are often at odds with the kinds of market behavior that trading systems are attempting to capitalize on (e.g., trend-following—a few large profits and many small losses). Due to this reality in performance numbers, sometimes system developers shy away from trend trading despite the overall superiority and psychological compatibility of these trading programs. System developers sometimes strive toward perfection in the performance results of their systems. Although it is satisfying to see smooth and even distributions of profits and losses in performance numbers, system developers should not sacrifice solid profits and modest drawdowns in favor of smoother distributions in performance results.

Such sacrifices are usually nothing more than another manifestation of the perfect trader syndrome. Instead of seeking unattainable perfection in profit and loss distribution, it is far better to choose robust trading systems that are attuned to our psychological center of gravity. By implementing trading systems that are most compatible with our individual personalities, we ensure the greatest likelihood of our adherence to the system's trading signals during its inevitable periods of equity drawdown.

DATA ANALYSIS PROCESS

Overview

Now that we have clearly established the limitations and benefits of various data analysis processes, we can examine the distinct levels of data analysis. Although there may be other methodologies by which to delineate our data, I have found that generally there are three different levels to data analysis of trading systems: analysis by asset classes, year-by-year analysis of in-sample data, and analysis of out-of-sample data.

Data Analysis by Asset Classes

For examples of analysis of data by asset classes, I refer the reader back to Tables 3.2 to 3.10. Ideally, system developers would like to see smooth and evenly distributed profits throughout all assets within these tables. However, it is more important that a system displays solid performance vis-à-vis risk than that such performance is evenly distributed throughout all assets in our backtested data history. With this caveat in mind, let us compare the various trading system results shown in Tables 3.2 to 3.10 and attempt to draw some conclusions regarding the data.

For now, we will narrow the field of study to those systems that generated a profit to maximum drawdown ratio of 3.0 or higher for the entire portfolio (shown here as Tables 7.21 to 7.25). Narrowing the field of study ensures that we do not waste our time and energy analyzing marginally performing trading systems, which we have no intention of trading in real time.

Table 7.21 not only generated the largest net profits, but it also exhibited the smoothest distribution of net profits among the various asset classes studied. Tables 7.22 and 7.23 also showed fairly smooth distributions of net profits throughout the various assets. Tables 7.24 and 7.25 are probably the most questionable of the tables analyzed in our asset-by-asset

TABLE 7.21 MACD.

Asset	Profit	# Trades	# Days	Max Draw	MDD	MCL	P:MD	P:L Ratio	%W	Time %
ES	−4242	19	133	−42446	1089	4	−0.10	0.91	36.84	100
TY	35678	19	132	−12875	810	5	2.77	3.10	47.37	100
ED	9097	15	165	−6812	1827	8	1.34	2.60	26.67	100
SF	58225	14	179	−20225	516	3	2.88	3.72	57.14	100
JY	37	18	137	−41500	1098	2	0.00	1.00	44.44	100
CL	61080	14	179	−19840	521	5	3.08	4.75	42.86	100
GC	740	22	113	−13810	985	6	0.05	1.04	36.36	100
S	−18812	23	110	−35325	2378	5	−0.53	0.61	34.78	100
LH	21440	18	139	−11690	688	4	1.83	1.94	50.00	100
CT	56255	13	193	−13990	510	1	4.02	6.43	61.54	100
Total	**219498**	**175**	**142.9**	**−42554**	**686**	**7**	**5.16**	**2.34**	**42.85**	**100**

Note: All trade summaries include $100 round-turn trade deductions for slippage and commissions. Data source: CQG, Inc.

TABLE 7.22 Two moving average crossover.

Asset	Profit	# Trades	# Days	Max Draw	MDD	MCL	P:MD	P:L Ratio	%W	Time %
ES	6023	117	22	(24621)	1122	7	0.24	1.07	35.90	100
TY	10678	94	27	(10681)	1032	5	1.00	1.18	37.23	100
ED	5952	88	28	(5606)	1577	9	1.06	1.41	32.95	100
SF	15650	121	22	(30350)	565	7	0.52	1.14	40.50	100
JY	66337	112	23	(33662)	1076	4	1.97	1.49	43.75	100
CL	27940	90	29	(16150)	566	5	1.73	1.45	42.22	100
GC	−13600	113	23	(23210)	2207	7	−0.59	0.73	36.28	100
S	−1162	103	25	(15612)	1596	8	−0.07	0.98	38.83	100
LH	43490	90	29	(10210)	530	7	4.26	2.03	46.67	100
CT	8155	110	23	(28870)	1946	7	0.28	1.09	34.55	100
Total	**169463**	**1038**	**24.8**	**−39954**	**635**	**10**	**4.24**	**1.23**	**38.82**	**100**

Note: All trade summaries include $100 round-turn trade deductions for slippage and commissions. Data source: CQG, Inc.

study. This is due to the fact that in both instances, one asset (IMM Japanese yen futures) represented over 50 percent of the total net profits generated by the entire portfolio during the backtested period.

Year-by-Year In-Sample Data Analysis

As with our examination of performance on an asset-by-asset basis, here again we do not want to sacrifice superior raw performance merely to en-

TABLE 7.23 Channel breakout.

Asset	Profit	# Trades	# Days	Max Draw	MDD	MCL	P:MD	P:L Ratio	%W	Time %
ES	11269	75	35	−27001	798	7	0.42	1.19	34.67	100
TY	28437	65	40	−15300	1252	5	1.86	1.67	43.08	100
ED	−4125	85	31	−10080	1903	9	−0.41	0.83	25.88	100
SF	27812	68	38	−17625	561	5	1.58	1.33	45.59	100
JY	63475	74	35	−20125	994	4	3.15	1.59	39.19	100
CL	8130	76	34	−23190	743	6	0.35	1.12	42.11	100
GC	−780	78	33	−9490	2250	7	−0.08	0.98	30.77	100
S	5337	78	33	−16375	1760	4	0.33	1.10	37.18	100
LH	36400	73	36	−10630	664	5	3.42	1.94	52.05	100
CT	−16920	87	30	−38060	1947	7	−0.44	0.83	28.74	100
Total	**159035**	**759**	**34.3**	**−44898**	**749**	**19**	**3.54**	**1.24**	**37.42**	**100**

Note: All trade summaries include $100 round-turn trade deductions for slippage and commissions. Data source: CQG, Inc.

TABLE 7.24 Three moving average Ichimoku crossover.

Asset	Profit	# Trades	# Days	Max Draw	MDD	MCL	P:MD	P:L Ratio	%W	Time %
ES	−17869	75	22	−9330	907	7	−0.57	0.75	30.67	62.44
TY	21525	56	30	−10931	556	4	1.97	1.61	42.86	64.97
ED	7471	58	32	−5106	1518	10	1.46	1.80	34.48	70.64
SF	32550	72	24	−11275	541	5	2.89	1.60	44.44	64.57
JY	81462	62	27	−16837	649	6	4.84	2.40	48.39	64.00
CL	9610	61	27	−21750	702	7	0.44	1.22	42.62	62.35
GC	−12680	73	22	−20560	2357	6	−0.62	0.65	32.88	61.45
S	−2800	64	25	−14712	2378	7	−0.19	0.93	34.37	61.80
LH	15690	63	26	−10610	1014	4	1.48	1.45	41.27	62.68
CT	18270	68	24	−16360	1946	8	1.12	1.38	36.76	62.58
Total	**153229**	**652**	**25.6**	**−50911**	**1168**	**10**	**3.01**	**1.35**	**38.65**	**63.62**

Note: All trade summaries include $100 round-turn trade deductions for slippage and commissions. Data source: CQG, Inc.

sure the smoothest year-by-year distribution of net profits. With this caveat in mind, we can proceed to analyze our backtested performance results for the trading systems studied in chapters three and four of the manuscript.

Table 7.26 provides us with a year-by-year breakdown of performance of the trend-following systems showcased in Chapter 3. Notice that in contrast to our asset class analysis, here I have retained marginal performing trading systems for illustrative purposes.

As expected, because all the systems in Chapter 3 employed trend-trading methodologies, most performed quite well in strongly trending years

TABLE 7.25 Bollinger bands.

Asset	Profit	# Trades	# Days	Max Draw	MDD	MCL	P:MD	P:L Ratio	%W	Time %
ES	−20113	97	13	−39957	1358	9	−0.50	0.71	36.08	44.72
TY	6195	97	15	−12296	2088	11	0.50	1.14	39.18	52.07
ED	1704	83	17	−6066	1783	10	0.28	1.15	33.73	53.40
SF	25486	91	15	−16374	1058	8	1.56	1.43	36.26	51.09
JY	67096	79	19	−11773	388	3	5.70	1.90	48.10	56.26
CL	7305	97	15	−12815	528	7	0.57	1.13	34.02	54.21
GC	−13157	96	15	−19969	2327	9	−0.66	0.65	29.17	50.32
S	−31	91	13	14914	1461	8	0.00	1.00	34.07	44.70
LH	14615	88	18	−16181	770	6	0.90	1.36	43.18	54.88
CT	18296	100	14	−24762	1947	9	0.74	1.31	34.00	51.36
Total	**107396**	**919**	**15.3**	**−28323**	**727**	**17**	**3.79**	**1.16**	**36.56**	**51.18**

Note: All trade summaries include $100 round-turn trade deductions for slippage and commissions. Data source: CQG, Inc.

(i.e., 1997 and 2001) and performed poorly in choppy years (2000). Here again the MACD trading system was superior in our year-by-year performance analysis. Notice how its losing years were clustered at the beginning of our study. Furthermore, the two most recent years in our backtested study (2001 and 2002) were among the best for the system. All of this suggests that the MACD trading system is robust enough to adapt successfully to recent market dynamics. By contrast, the results produced by the two moving average Ichimoku crossover system are highly suspect because four of the seven most recent years in our backtested period were losers and the system produced an overall net loss of $37,980.00 from January 1, 1996, to December 31, 2002.

Table 7.27 provides us with a year-by-year breakdown of performance of the mean reversion trading systems showcased in Chapter 4. Although I address issues of system diversification extensively in Chapter 9, for now let us examine each system's year-by-year performance and then touch briefly on how these results compare with those of Table 7.26.

Table 7.27's most robust performance was produced by the RSI extremes with 200-day moving average filter applied to our mean reversion portfolio of assets (see Chapter 4 for a more detailed explanation of the system). Although this system did produce a loss in 2001, the most recent year's performance (2002) was its most profitable. Furthermore, looking back at the year 2001 performance for the trend trading systems in Table 7.26, it is clear that the performance of RSI extremes for the mean reversion portfolio failed for all the "right" reasons. In other words, it failed because the markets were in a strong trending mode. In this type of environment we should expect a mean reversion system to experience a losing year.

TABLE 7.26 Year-by-year performance breakdown for trend-following systems of Chapter 3.

System	1993	1994	1995	1996	1997	1998	1999	2000	2001	2002
2 MA Crossover	(14439)	14745	78166	11436	27080	1553	13750	(1862)	31692	(871)
2 MA Ichimoku	18314	33367	11021	(49435)	16080	(3296)	(47343)	(27508)	28491	45031
3 MA Crossover	10028	422	67858	12717	20045	11318	12396	(30198)	19088	14298
3 MA Ichimoku	10941	8794	69736	17769	22736	8214	18350	(32851)	17050	12088
MACD	(5359)	(2250)	(28318)	30953	107917	3640	8766	3713	39199	67199
DMI	(13029)	(4864)	20255	13943	20361	1935	(917)	(17876)	13281	29372
DMI with ADX filter	(10748)	(4174)	19921	9731	12730	(846)	1753	(15781)	15219	30916
Channel Breakout	(17181)	8478	16026	42582	14906	30626	13813	(18640)	43025	26356
Bollinger Bands	2257	12083	28191	9469	5734	19940	(5044)	(11906)	18385	28287

Note: All trade summaries include $100 round-turn trade deductions for slippage and commissions. Data source: CQG, Inc.

TABLE 7.27 Year-by-year performance breakdown for mean reversion systems of Chapter 4.

System	1993	1994	1995	1996	1997	1998	1999	2000	2001	2002
RSI with 200 day MA Futures	7060	(11686)	9610	26221	2812	7226	(2867)	(10284)	(6678)	908
RSI with 200 day MA	(11485)	30379	17304	11724	3946	3179	11995	14815	(22996)	43021
Bollinger Bands with 200 day MA	(14153)	4098	9043	697	26164	6706	2577	(12116)	15831	12248
Bollinger Bands with ADX filter	(209)	(1516)	4838	(3758)	4616	7883	(7702)	3082	12817	3219
Slow Stochastics & CCI	(10607)	3416	(3206)	(10818)	(6564)	18462	17777	13765	(4691)	1691
Slow Stochastics & CCI with Time Exit	(11397)	4674	(4845)	(9669)	(4954)	16596	17234	14499	(829)	231

Note: All trade summaries include $100 round-turn trade deductions for slippage and commissions. Data source: CQG, Inc.

Now let us examine our worst-performing mean reversion system results. Interestingly, the worst performer (RSI extremes with 200-day moving average applied to the futures portfolio) utilized the same exact trade execution criteria as our best-performing system (RSI extremes with 200-day moving average applied to the mean reversion portfolio). This warns us that the mean reversion systems examined in Chapter 4 were not robust enough to be successful across a diversified group of asset classes. This fact is clearly highlighted by the failure of the futures portfolio from January 1, 1999, to the end of our in-sample test period on December 31, 2002.

Although this does suggest a higher degree of overall confidence in the trend-following systems of Chapter 3, the matter is not as cut and dried as might appear, due to the negative correlation between mean reversion and trend-following systems. The poor performance of RSI extremes on our mean reversion portfolio in 2001 was in stark contrast to the strong results displayed by the trend-following systems that year. Perhaps more important, a comparison of Tables 7.26 and 7.27 shows positive performance by our mean reversion system during the year 2000, which was our worst year for the trend trading systems.

Out-of-Sample Data Analysis

A case study based on one of the trading systems from Chapter 3 may be instructive. Table 7.28 is an out-of-sample data analysis for the two moving average crossover system. Table 7.22 showed in-sample data for this system. If we compare the out-of-sample data from 2003 to our in-sample

TABLE 7.28 Out-of-sample (2003) performance for two moving average crossover system.

Asset	Profit	# Trades	# Days	Max Draw	MDD	MCL	P:MD	P:L Ratio	%W	Time %
ES	224	9	32	−6617	96	3	0.03	1.02	33.33	100
TY	3141	10	26	−6619	60	2	0.47	1.48	40.00	100
ED	−2619	12	19	−2737	215	8	−0.96	0.02	8.33	100
SF	5000	10	23	−9162	52	2	0.55	1.70	50.00	100
JY	−1662	12	22	−11537	220	7	−0.14	0.86	25.00	100
CL	−2880	8	27	−9920	98	3	−0.29	0.68	37.50	100
GC	5820	6	38	−3690	63	1	1.58	4.20	66.67	100
S	−2125	15	19	−10800	175	6	−0.20	0.84	13.33	100
LH	5170	8	37	−2770	51	2	1.87	3.62	75.00	100
CT	2560	9	32	−7735	183	4	0.33	1.32	44.44	100
Total	**12629**	**99**	**26**	**−24647**	**70**	**7**	**0.51**	**1.37**	**35.35**	**100**

Note: All trade summaries include $100 round-turn trade deductions for slippage and commissions. Data source: CQG, Inc.

calendar years (see Table 7.26), it appears that our total net profit is well within normal tolerances. But what if total net profits were dramatically different from those of our in-sample backtest? If our 2003 results were 50 percent worse than the system's performance in 1993, the system should be abandoned because of the high probability of paradigm shift in markets as stated in our first examination of the out-of-sample study.

If, however, we had seen a total net profit that exceeded our 1995 results by more than 150 percent, we would need to carefully examine such performance in attempt to ascertain whether the markets had undergone a paradigm shift.[18] Although additional analysis in the face of such extraordinary profits seems counterintuitive, unprecedented profitability is likely to have been a byproduct of increased volatility (defined as the speed and magnitude of price movement).

Analyzing severe increases in volatility is not as simple as it might appear. The difficulty stems from the fact that volatility tends to trend and that it exhibits heteroskedasticity. (Heteroskedasticity means that volatility is not constant, but instead that it tends to cycle from periods of high volatility to low volatility ad infinitum.) Consequently, as long as the trend of volatility remains intact, we should reduce our position size to stay within prudent price risk management tolerances (see Chapter 8). However, once the uptrend in volatility has been violated, we can expect a cycle of low volatility to ensue, and so the position size assumptions established during our in-sample backtest are likely to be satisfactory.

The study of the volatility trend of a single asset can prove to be a daunting task, and application of those principles to an entire portfolio of diversified assets often is nightmarish. Thus, unless a person is a risk manager for a large financial institution with sophisticated software for analyzing volatility trends, it is prudent to scale back position size to stay within price risk management tolerances dictated by the out-of-sample results.

The other comparisons between our in-sample and out-of-sample data include categories such as maximum drawdown, profit to maximum drawdown, average trade duration, and win/loss ratio. Scanning through the "totals" rows of Tables 7.22 and 7.28 reinforces our initial year-by-year conclusions regarding the acceptability of the out-of-sample results.

Other interesting points to note in the out-of-sample results are the poor performance of IMM Japanese yen in 2003 and the stellar performance of Comex gold in this same year. Both performances were atypical based on nearly all of the in-sample studies shown in Chapter 3. I point this out to reinforce the importance of maintaining a diversified portfolio. The markets are *not* going to behave the same in the future as they have in the past. As a result, cherry picking certain asset classes in hopes of improving performance sometimes can lead to disastrous results.

TRADING SYSTEM PHILOSOPHY STATEMENTS

Most asset allocation firms and many institutional investors will ask traders for a trading methodology philosophy statement along with hypothetical and real-time trading results. I encourage traders and system developers to write a philosophy statement for each of their trading systems (and for their combined portfolio of systems, if applicable), irrespective of whether they are currently attempting to secure outside allocations of capital. By formulating a trading philosophy statement, we concretize trading strategies and/or mechanics and sometimes can identify flaws in logic or price risk management prior to committing capital in the markets. In addition, this document serves as an ideological benchmark of performance expectations through which we can compare our real-time results. The philosophy statement should include these items.

- *Overall trading philosophy.* The philosophy statement should outline explicitly the principles on which the strategy is based, what type of market behavior the methodology is attempting to capitalize on (e.g., trend-following or mean reversion), and why it is robust enough for similar results to be achieved in the future.
- *Length of performance (and/or backtested) history.* This section should explain to potential investors the length of performance (and/or backtested) history. The explanation should prove that the data history is robust enough to include all types of market environments (bullish, bearish, trending, choppy, volatile and neutral). In addition, the data history should include enough trades to be statistically significant.
- *Liquidity risk.* This section should include all assumptions regarding liquidity of the markets traded. It must detail allowances for round-turn slippage and/or commissions. Regardless of the superior liquidity of the assets traded, I always assume a minimum deduction of $75 per round-turn trade and routinely increase this assumption to $200 per round-turn trade for many of the asset classes highlighted in Chapters 3 and 4.
- *Trade duration and average flat time.* This section should include the estimated average duration of trades. Often I break this section down into average duration of winning and of losing trades. Familiarity with this measure sometimes can clue us in to paradigm shifts in market behavior.

    Inclusion of average flat time shows prospective investors how actively their account will be traded. Like trade duration, it is also valuable in alerting traders to shifts in market behavior.
- *Stop losses.* Without disclosing the detailed mechanics of our trading system, the philosophy statement should let potential investors know

how stops are triggered (e.g., based on a percentage of asset value at time of entry, fixed dollar amounts, etc.). Traders using fixed dollar amounts must include a detailed review process for adjusting these amounts as volatility of the portfolio (or asset) rises/falls.

- *Maximum consecutive losses.* Inclusion of this number psychologically prepares investors for weathering the inevitable string of losses inherent in execution of any trading strategy. It can also clue traders in to a shift in market dynamics so that we can adjust or possibly abandon our trading system.

- *Price risk management.* This section should include assumptions regarding worst peak-to-valley drawdowns in equity, allowances for exceeding worst peak-to-valley drawdown assumptions (typically a 50 percent increase over the largest historical drawdown), and a stop loss for the trading system. Chapter 8 addresses the issue of trading system stop losses in greater detail; the basic idea is adherence to a maximum peak-to-valley drawdown for the trading system (37.5 percent of equity under management is a popular system stop-loss level for trading systems). Violation of this peak-to-valley drawdown percentage will result in liquidation of the fund (or trading account).

The worst peak-to-valley drawdown number should be broken down into two subcategories—worst monthly peak-to-valley drawdown and maximum peak-to-valley drawdown—which could encompass several calendar months. Exclusion of this second measurement masks the true risk of the trading system.

Finally, this section should include the maximum duration of drawdowns. This performance measure psychologically clues investors in to the amount of time that they can expect to hold their investment without experiencing a new high water mark in account equity. As with many of the other measures covered in the philosophy statement, significant deviations in durations of drawdowns are also instructive as they can alert traders to fundamental shifts in market behavior.

MEASURING TRADING SYSTEM PERFORMANCE

The Sharpe ratio continues to be the traditional and standard measure of performance of both managed funds and trading systems. This ratio is defined as the expected return minus the risk-free interest rate (e.g., treasury bills[20]) divided by the standard deviation of returns. The "expected return" is defined as the average past return of the entire data sampling in question. Standard deviation is a statistical measure of volatility of the entire data history. It measures the degree of dispersion of the individual data points in the history from the mean (or average) of that history. High standard deviation (high volatility) occurs when many of the individual time intervals within the history deviate dramatically from the average past return for the period.

My objective is not to provide a comprehensive exposition of all the shortcomings of the Sharpe ratio, but rather to outline some of the most dangerous flaws in utilizing this ratio to the exclusion of other measures of system performance.[21] The basic premise of the Sharpe ratio is that the wider dispersal of individual returns from the average past return, the riskier the investment. Although it is true that a wider dispersal of individual returns from the average past return does suggest higher volatility, because the Sharpe ratio makes no distinction between profits and losses in the composition of its measure of volatility, high volatility of returns does not necessarily equate to a riskier investment. Because the ratio cannot distinguish between upside and downside fluctuations in performance histories, it tends to penalize successful trend traders, because typically they experience dramatic increases in account equity followed by small retracements.

In addition, the Sharpe ratio does not distinguish between intermittent losses and consecutive losses; instead, it measures only the standard deviation of returns for the period analyzed. For example, say Trading System A generates three consecutive monthly losses of $4,000, followed by nine consecutive monthly gains of $3,500 for a total annual profit of $19,500, and Trading System B alternates between monthly profits of $7,500 and losses of $3,750 for a total annual profit of $22,500. Because the Sharpe ratio does not distinguish between intermittent and consecutive losses and because it cannot distinguish between upside and downside fluctuations in the performance history, it will show Trading System A as the superior trading vehicle despite the fact that System A had to endure a $12,000 drawdown in equity and enjoyed a lower average annualized return on investment.

By contrast, the profit to maximum drawdown ratio (P:MD) utilized throughout this book does distinguish between upside and downside volatility while simultaneously punishing systems (and managers) that endure large consecutive losses. Despite the superiority of the profit to maximum drawdown ratio as a measure of system performance, Sharpe ratio continues to be the industrywide standard.

Consequently, I strongly recommend that the Sharpe ratio be included in traders' performance results while it is simultaneously supplemented by the more robust measure of the profit to maximum drawdown ratio. Because the P:MD is not yet a universally accepted measure of system analysis, the trading philosophy statement should explain why the P:MD ratio is included and why it gives a more comprehensive exposition of the true risk/reward dynamics of the system's performance.

CHAPTER 8

Price Risk Management

Schools of Price Risk Management and other Considerations

I'm not afraid of storms, for I'm learning how to sail my ship.

—Louisa May Alcott

PRICE RISK MANAGEMENT ISSUES: AN OVERVIEW

Although price risk management will not turn a losing trading strategy into a winner, it is arguably the most important topic in this book because it can prevent the failure of an overall profitable trading system. Imagine a system that produces an astonishing 90 percent win/loss ratio, and pair this system with a trader who commits all accumulated profits—along with the original stake—to the next trade. According to the laws of probability, on average, such a trader would end up broke by the termination of the tenth position.

The other reason why I believe price risk management is such an important tool in the trader's arsenal is that we can never control the markets, only how much risk we will assume in them. Because we can never know with certainty whether any particular trade will result in a profit or a loss, it is the height of folly to focus our attention and capital on those aspects of trading over which we have no control while simultaneously neglecting price risk management, the one essential aspect of trading over which we exercise absolute control.

Of course, we do also have control over which entry point we choose for any particular trade. However, the selection of precise entry levels probably represents the least significant aspect of a successful trading system. In his book, *Trade Your Way to Financial Freedom*, Van Tharp illustrates the lack of importance of precise price entry levels chosen in the development of a successful trading methodology by outlining a system Tom Basso, a trader interviewed in Schwager's *The New Market Wizards*, developed based on random entry signals.[1] Nevertheless, novice traders and system developers continue to focus their attention almost exclusively on selection of trade entry points because it represents their "control" in the markets; simultaneously they ignore the psychologically uncomfortable issue of losses and price risk management.

Many books on trading, system development, and technical analysis include sections entitled "Risk Management." In reality, these books almost always are referring to the need to manage a specific type of risk, namely, price risk. Market participants need to manage various other types of risk as well. Some, such as liquidity risk, are addressed in this chapter, due to their critical and universal effect on issues of price risk management. For a discussion of other types of risk management, such as credit and operational risk management, see *Risk Management* by Crouhy, Galai, and Mark.

During the early years of my career as a trader, Refco, one of the larger exchange-traded derivatives brokers, used "Risk Is Everywhere" as its advertising slogan. I have always liked the phrase because it succinctly dispels one of the great myths of investing, namely, that we can somehow avoid financial risk. This myth suggests that investment vehicles that do not guarantee a return of principal are risky and that we can somehow avoid risk by putting our money under the mattresses, in a bank, or in T-bills. Obviously, investing in vehicles that do not guarantee a return of principal entails greater risk than those that do; however, in choosing investment vehicles like T-bills, we end up accepting the opportunity risk inherent in our forfeiting a potentially higher rate of return.

This comparison of guaranteed return of principal investment vehicles with "riskier" investment alternatives illuminates an inescapable law of investment: The higher the risk, the greater the reward (and conversely, the lower the risk, the lower the reward). Promises of high reward and low risk suggest three possibilities:

1. The probability of realizing this high reward is remote enough to compensate for its relatively low level of financial risk (e.g., lottery tickets, deep out-of-the-money options, etc.).

2. The entity proposing the investment lacks a fundamental understanding of the true risk/reward entailed in the investment vehicle.

3. The entity proposing the investment understands the true risk/reward but is attempting to hide these realities (e.g., fraud, money laundering, etc.) from prospective investor(s).

STOP-LOSS PRICE RISK MANAGEMENT FOR TRADING ACCOUNTS

Obviously traders can improve their system's rate of return simply by increasing the worst peak-to-valley drawdown levels allowable. For example, let us assume $100,000 under management and that our trading system executes single contract positions on a given portfolio. Based on this criterion, we discover that our system endured a worst peak-to-valley drawdown of $20,000 or 20 percent for our portfolio. Consequently, as long as we are willing to weather a 40 percent worst peak-to-valley drawdown in equity, we could double our average annualized rate of return simply by trading two contacts instead of one.

Although this may sound tempting, it is important to remember that the higher the peak-to-valley drawdown we experience, the lower our system's likelihood of profitability. The probability of our returning to profitability decreases exponentially as the percentage of peak-to-valley drawdowns in equity increase. For example, a peak-to-valley drawdown in equity of 15 percent would require a subsequent gain of 17.6 percent to recapture the break-even level. By contrast, a 50 percent peak-to-valley drawdown in equity requires a gain of 100 percent to regain the break-even level. Furthermore, this subsequent 100 percent gain would need to be accomplished with one-half of the original equity under management. The likelihood of a 100 percent gain in equity, after experiencing a 50 percent peak-to-valley equity drawdown, is so remote that some hedge funds employ a fund stop-loss level of 37.5 percent drawdown from the most recent equity peak.[2]

As a result, designation of a stop-loss level for the trading account or trading system is an unyielding prerequisite for successful price risk management. So how do we minimize our chances of ever experiencing a 37.5 percent drawdown in equity? We will seek to answer throughout the remainder of this chapter, but one commonly employed (although incomplete) solution adapted by system developers is to examine the worst drawdown of the backtested period and allow for a drawdown that exceeds this level by 50 percent. Based on this reasoning, if the worst drawdown of our backtested history was 20 percent, we should be prepared to endure a 30 percent drawdown and adjust our volumetric position sizing limits accordingly.

TWO SCHOOLS OF PRICE RISK MANAGEMENT

Read enough books on trading and price risk management, and one may come to the erroneous conclusion that there are two distinct schools of price risk management: trader school and VaR/stress testing school. Although both schools sometimes imagine their theories regarding price risk management to be mutually exclusive, usually this is not the case. Furthermore, it is only through adaptation of the strengths of both approaches that a robust price risk management solution can be achieved.

One school dominates the books that have been written by and for traders. These books typically emphasize managing price risk based on two factors:

1. Volumetric price risk management, which is based on the size of the positions taken in the markets or how many volumetric units (e.g., contracts, shares, etc.) will be traded

2. Stop-loss price risk management, which determines the size of the risk assumed per position traded or how much capital will be risked per volumetric unit traded

The other school is composed primarily of risk management professionals and academicians who focus on price risk management on a portfolio-wide basis and utilize tools such as value at risk (VaR) and stress testing to aid in their development of a comprehensive price risk management strategy. VaR examines the standard deviation (or historical volatility) of a trading portfolio as well as the correlations between its various components. Stress testing attempts to illuminate weaknesses in VaR studies by analyzing the potential effect of price shocks and correlation breakdowns on the traded portfolio.

Although not always explicitly stated by the trader school of price risk management, both methods tend to measure price risk based on historical data. This is the reason why it is essential to ensure data integrity and robustness of trading systems and why I provided an in-depth explanation of these system development issues. Because both schools rely so heavily on historical data in developing price risk management strategies and because the markets will never behave exactly the same in the future as they have in the past, we must continuously assess and reassess future price risk.

STOP-LOSS PRICE RISK MANAGEMENT

Perhaps one of the most effective and fundamental aspects of managing price risk is the placement of stop-loss orders on a per-trade basis. Stop-loss placement forces us to exit positions when the market is no longer behaving as our trading models anticipated. Although there are no absolute answers regarding the placement of our stop-loss orders, it is generally agreed that they should be far enough from the current market price to prevent "normal" fluctuations from resulting in realized losses, without being placed so far away that their election would result in endurance of a loss that jeopardizes our ability to return to profitability.

Studies of recent volatility on the markets traded, for our specific trading time frames, are probably the single most important element in successful minimization of losses due to normal market fluctuations. The second aspect of stop-loss placement, the jeopardizing of our ability to return to profitability, requires that this market volatility analysis be reviewed in relation to our total equity under management.

For example, if typical recent volatility levels on IMM Japanese yen futures for our specified trading time frame suggest that stop-loss orders should be no less than $1,500 from entry price, then the Japanese yen is probably an appropriate trading vehicle if our equity under management were $100,000, because one contract would represent 1.5 percent risk of total equity under management (generally considered an acceptable level of per-position risk). On the other hand, if our equity under management were $15,000, then taking a position in the Japanese yen would represent an unacceptable level of price risk, because one contract would now represent 10 percent risk of total equity under management.

Just as there are no absolute answers regarding the placement of stop-loss orders, neither are there any absolute answers regarding maximum levels of total per-position risk. The issue is made even more complicated by the fact that certain assets and/or trading systems may have positive or negative correlations to existing positions currently held in our trading accounts. If open positions have a positive correlation to our potential entry signal, prudent price risk management might suggest that we avoid trade execution despite our having adequate funds for the trade on a stand-alone basis. For example, if we currently held an open long position in Chicago Board of Trade (CBOT) soybeans, our purchase of CBOT soybean meal might represent excessive risk due to the strong positive correlation between these markets. By contrast, if we held the same long CBOT soybeans position and received a sell signal in CBOT soybean meal, because of this same strong positive correlation between these assets, it might be prudent to take the soybean meal trade even if that trade's stand-alone risk seemed excessive.

Aside from these correlation considerations, a good general rule of thumb is to limit per-position exposure to somewhere between 1 and 2 percent of our total equity under management. Why 1 to 2 percent? Because our goal is to ensure that our account will be able to survive long enough to return to profitability after enduring our worst equity drawdown. Remember the 37.5 percent trading account stop-loss level? Well, the lower our percentage of equity stop-loss on a per-trade basis, the lower the probability of triggering the 37.5 percent trading account stop-loss level. If we assume

$100,000 in equity under management and set our per-trade stop-loss level at 4 percent, it would mean that 12 consecutive losses[3] would trigger our trading account stop loss (see maximum consecutive loss columns of Tables 3.9 and 3.10). By contrast, if we had $100,000 in equity under management and set our per-trade stop-loss level at 1 percent, it would translate into having to endure 47 consecutive losses before activating our 37.5 percent trading account stop loss.

Finally, the ability to quantify per-position risk in relation to equity under management is particularly useful for traders utilizing leveraged instruments, such as futures and/or options. This is due to the fact that per-position risk in relation to total equity under management negates questions of leverage and margin, and instead allows the manager to trade as many contracts as desired, so long as they do not exceed the 1 to 2 percent limit on a per-position basis.

VOLUMETRIC PRICE RISK MANAGEMENT: MARTINGALE AND ANTI-MARTINGALE STRATEGIES

Stop-loss price risk management is not, in and of itself, a sufficient risk management methodology and should be complemented by a robust system of designating stop-loss levels per volumetric position(s) taken. This two-tiered approach to price risk management allows us to answer these questions: How much I am willing to risk on a per unit basis (stop-loss limit level)? and How many units I am willing to trade on a per account basis (volumetric limit level)?

Although there are infinite varieties of volumetric price risk management strategies, all of them can be broken down into two basic philosophies of position sizing: Martingale and anti-Martingale. Martingale is a method in which the volumetric size of the risks assumed are doubled after every losing trade. The theory is that if we merely continue to double our position size after every loss, eventually we will regain everything lost in addition to the original stake. The problem with Martingale is that a string of consecutive losses will result in bankruptcy. If our beginning position size risked $1,000, 11 consecutive losses utilizing a Martingale strategy would result in a drawdown in account equity of over $1 million. A review of the performance tables 3.9, 3.10, and 4.4 shows that, although a rarity, 11 consecutive losses will occur for some moderately successful trading systems.

Although a "pure" Martingale position sizing methodology is defined as the doubling of volumetric exposure after every loss, participants in the financial markets commonly employ other, equally lethal varieties of such adding-to-losses strategies. The most popular of these strategies—typically employed on the long side of the equities markets—is known as *averaging down*. In contrast to doubling the volumetric risk after each loss, those employing averaging down strategies double their existing volumetric exposure on losing positions whenever the position held loses half of its value. A common stock shifting from growth to bankruptcy reveals the inherent flaw in utilization of such a strategy.

Because Martingale and Martingale look-alikes, such as averaging down, are disastrous as volumetric risk management methodologies, strategies that increase volumetric exposure during and/or after increases in equity under management should provide us with an attractive alternative. Such strategies are collectively known as *anti-Martingale* methods. The most simplistic anti-Martingale technique would entail doubling our position size after each gain and returning to our original volumetric exposure after a loss. Although such a position sizing technique might be robust enough to be effective in price risk arenas in which per-position profits and losses were identical, the technique is generally considered a suboptimal answer to the issue of volumetric price risk management in the financial markets because of the nature of trading strategies employed (e.g., trend-following—inequality of profits and losses) as well as the heteroskedasticity of the assets traded.

A more robust anti-Martingale methodology is known as fixed fractional money management. The basic premise behind fixed fractional money management is that volumetric exposure increases or decreases as equity under management fluctuates. For example, if we were trading a system that experienced a worst peak-to-valley drawdown in equity of $10,000 on a $100,000 portfolio during the backtested period and we intended to trade this system with $1,000,000 under management, we could trade 10 contracts for each signal generated while still retaining the expectation of a worst peak-to-valley drawdown in equity of 10 percent. Once our account equity increased to $1,100,000 we could increase our position size to 11 contracts while retaining the same 10 percent worst peak-to-valley expectation. On the other hand, a decrease in equity to $900,000 would force a reduction of our position size to 9 contracts to retain this same 10 percent worst peak-to-valley drawdown expectation.

One of the major benefits in utilizing the fixed fractional money management methodology is that it forces both a slowing of the rate of equity deterioration during drawdowns and simultaneously accelerates market exposure during periods of increases in account equity.[4]

VALUE AT RISK: AN OVERVIEW

Although an in-depth discussion of the various methods of calculating VaR is beyond the scope of this book, I will provide a general overview of the topic and why it is an important complement to traditional methods of price risk management (e.g., stop-loss and volumetric price risk management).[5]

Value-at-risk methodologies attempt to quantify the standard deviation (or historical volatility) of a trading asset or portfolio of assets and the historical correlations between these assets in order to answer the question: What is the likelihood of our losing X dollars or more over a specified time horizon under normal market conditions?" For example, a particular hedge fund might have a daily VaR of $30 million at the 95 percent confidence level. This would translate into there being a 95 percent probability of the portfolio not experiencing a loss in excess of $30 million over the next 24 hours.

BENEFITS OF VALUE AT RISK

Although VaR provides traders and risk managers with a multitude of benefits, its most touted benefit—the introduction of probability of loss for a given portfolio over a specified future time horizon—is applicable to all market participants. The key feature here is VaR's incorporation of historical volatility and correlations for a specific portfolio to forecast future price risk with some notion of likelihood over a given holding period.

Risk managers and system developers utilizing traditional measures such as stop-loss and volumetric price risk analysis can tell us many essential aspects of portfolio risk, such as the likelihood of an account trading specific assets with a particular methodology experiencing a 20 percent peak-to-valley drawdown over the course of the past 10 years. Moreover, they can determine how many times such an account would have endured daily losses in excess of a particular monetary threshold (e.g., $10 million). In fact, this ability to determine the number of times that a portfolio experienced a daily loss in excess of $10 million is a nonstatistically based VaR methodology known as historical VaR.

Historical VaR allows us to establish some notion of probability in regard to losses over a given historical time horizon (such as one year) simply by counting off the worst occurrences of the trading account until we have identified the desired percentage of largest losing trading days. For example, if last year contained 255 trading days and we were interested in determining the historical VaR for a trading account with a 95 percent probability or confidence level over a 24-hour holding period, we could simply count off the 13 days in which that account experienced its largest daily losses. This is because 5 percent times 255 trading days gives us roughly 13 trading days for the calendar year in question. As a result, if last year's thirteenth least severe daily loss was $5 million and last year's average daily trading result was a profit of $2.5 million, then the historical VaR for last year would be $7.5 million.

Unfortunately, neither historical VaR nor traditional price risk management tools tell us anything regarding the probability of losses over the next 24 hours for our current portfolio holdings. By contrast, forward-looking (parametric and simulation) VaR models apply statistical measures, such as standard deviation and correlations, to current portfolio holdings to estimate probability distributions of losses for a particular holding period (i.e., 24 hours). Subsequently, forward-looking VaR models can effectively account for how the addition of a particular position to current portfolio holdings will either reduce or increase portfolio risk (due to its negative or positive correlation to the existing portfolio).[6]

PITFALLS OF VALUE AT RISK

Although value at risk is a valuable tool, it does not provide a comprehensive solution to the problem of managing price risk. This is because VaR does not address how much we could lose during a given holding period, only the maximum that we are *likely* to lose. For example, while VaR defines an excessive loss for our particular trading account as $30 million and tells us that we have a 5 percent chance of enduring such a loss over the next 24 hours, it says nothing about how severely any particular daily loss will exceed this $30 million threshold.

Another flaw in VaR models is that they assume serial independence: whatever happened today has no impact on tomorrow's trading. Because all of the trading systems discussed in this text owed their success to the market's propensity to either trend or revert to the mean, serial independence is a flawed assumption.

The assumption of serial independence leads to VaR's inability to account for excessive event clusterings. For example, the fact that we exceeded our daily VaR threshold yesterday says nothing about the likelihood of VaR being exceeded again today. In fact, excessive event clusterings can be one of the distinguishing traits of a strongly trending market. This is perhaps best exemplified by the 1995 Mexican peso crisis, during which the market experienced 9 days beyond 20 standard deviations from the mean.

A subtler problem relating to cumulative losses is that VaR only attempts to predict the likelihood of violating a particular confidence level, such as 95 percent. Consequently, VaR cannot account for cumulative losses that never achieve the chosen VaR confidence threshold. This problem of cumulative daily losses below the VaR threshold is another example why traditional price risk management tools such as historical studies of worst peak-to-valley drawdowns, are an essential adjunct to VaR analysis.

Perhaps one of the most dangerous and flawed assumptions inherent in all VaR models is the ability of traders to close out positions without significant slippage. VaR literally "assumes away" liquidity risk, which is especially dangerous when we remember that this assumption of liquidity is being paired with an attempt to measure the probability of our trading account enduring an excessive and statistically improbable daily loss. We need only to imagine a commodity market in "locked limit" or recall the illiquidity of global equity markets on October 19, 1987, to see the disastrous potential of assuming away liquidity risk.

Finally, VaR assumes that correlation history is predictive. Just as we saw in the examination of VaR and liquidity, the pairing of historical correlations with a price shock event could lead to potentially fatal assumptions regarding price risk of a particular portfolio. In fact, one of the major distinguishing traits of a price shock event is the breakdown of historically stable correlations. This is perhaps best exemplified by the breakdown of the historically stable exchange rate relationship between the British pound and German deutsche mark during the Exchange Rate Mechanism (ERM) crisis in September 1992 (see Figure 8.1).

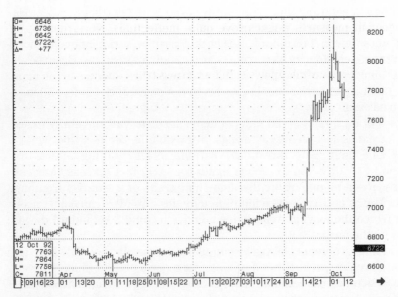

FIGURE 8.1 Daily chart of spot DM-pound preceding and during the 1992 ERM crisis.

STRESS TESTING

Stress testing attempts to address many of the flaws inherent in VaR exercises. Value at risk tries to quantify the likelihood of our portfolio's breaching of a particular loss threshold over a specified time horizon, but says nothing regarding the degree of severity of a particular loss. Stress testing attempts to quantify how bad the unlikely event could get, but—for the most part—fails to examine the probability of the particular event's occurrence. As such, stress tests are ideal complements to VaR analyses.

A comprehensive examination of stress testing methodologies is beyond the scope of this text.[7] However, an example will explain the basic concept and its utility. One of the simplest and most popular types of stress tests is known as scenario analysis. In scenario analysis, we apply to our current portfolio holdings either a hypothetical scenario, such as a 100 basis point rise in interest rates, or an actual historical scenario, such as the stock market crash of 1987, to determine our portfolio's vulnerability. Once our stress test has identified such portfolio hot spots, we can reduce these exposures by reducing position exposures or purchasing options.

Of course, stress testing has its own weaknesses, including the fact that neither hypothetical nor historical scenarios has any significant chance of resembling actual future price shock events (and therefore our protective risk management measures might prove quite ineffectual). Nevertheless, because stress testing can incorporate breakdowns in historical correlations, liquidity risk, cumulative losses, and clustering, it remains particularly valuable as an adjunct to VaR analysis. In fact, stress testing compensates for so many weaknesses in VaR methodologies that together it and VaR are viewed as two halves of a single school of price risk management.

PSYCHOLOGY OF PRICE RISK MANAGEMENT

Because the amount of risk that we are willing to assume is the only essential aspect of trading over which we exercise complete control, we can never be too diligent regarding price risk management. Why do successful hedge fund managers consistently show average annualized returns of between 5 and 25 percent? Obviously they could show average annualized returns of 50 to 250 percent, but this would greatly enhance their likelihood of ruin. One of the most common reasons retail and institutional traders fail is their lack of adherence to comprehensive, systematized price risk methodologies. This lack of adherence invariably manifests itself through their overleveraging of equity under management.

Although other factors may lead to our inability to "pull the trigger" on a trade, one of the most prevalent and sensible reasons is that we are risking too high a percentage of our total equity on a per-position basis. We should be hesitant to execute a trade if such an action could lead to the end of our careers as traders. This is simple self-preservation. If, prior to execution of a trade, traders are overwhelmed with anxiety, they should ask themselves if suffering a loss on this anticipated position would impede their financial ability to trade in the future. If the answer is yes, they should trade small enough to ensure that this would not be the case.

Our culture thrives on immediate gratification. Microwave ovens, airplanes, fad diets, T1 lines, fast food restaurants, and the like all address this need for speedy solutions. Part of the attraction to leveraged financial instruments is their ability to satiate our greed and impatience as traders by getting us rich quicker. Instead I admonish readers to get rich slowly and safely. Compare the rate of return on leveraged instruments to those of competitive investment vehicles. If it is considerably greater, compare the risk of ruin. Ideally, prudent price risk management should reduce the risk of ruin on leveraged assets to a level similar to that of nonleveraged instruments.

Other techniques to aid with the psychological problem of trigger pulling include risking only that capital that we truly do not care about losing. Only risking capital we can afford to lose is actually quite similar to a disclaimer adopted by brokerage firms making markets in leveraged instruments. It is much easier to practice nonattachment to the results of our actions in the market when we are not emotionally or psychologically attached to the funds being placed at risk at the endeavor's outset.

Prior to our assumption of a position in the markets, we should be able to answer these questions in the positive: Do I have adequate capital under management to weather a peak-to-valley drawdown in excess of the worst severity shown throughout my system's backtested history? Have I accounted for slippage/commissions in the event of a price shock event? Am I psychologically and financially prepared to exceed the largest number of consecutive losses endured by my system during its backtested history?

MECHANICAL TRADING SYSTEMS, DRAWDOWNS, AND TRADER CONFIDENCE

Mechanical trading systems can prove invaluable in the implementation of the various price risk management tools discussed in this chapter. Because such systems enable us to quantify risk on both a per-asset as well as a portfolio-wide basis, they are essential in the establishment of stop-loss levels, volumetric position sizing limits, and risk/reward estimates. Another, perhaps even more important benefit of mechanical trading systems is their ability to instill trader confidence during periods of equity drawdowns.

Drawdowns in equity under management are a fact of life for all traders. How traders handle these tough times ultimately will determine the degree of success that they and their portfolios will enjoy. A key to successful trading during equity drawdowns is the maintenance of consistency and discipline. Although it is never easy for traders to stick to rules of entry, exit, and risk management after suffering a string of losses, because mechanical trading systems are backtested prior to the commitment of capital, both portfolio managers and the investors they represent should enjoy greater confidence and tempered emotionalism during these inevitable periods of drawdowns in equity.

In fact, it is quite common for asset allocators to dedicate additional funds to a trading system that is in the midst of a sizable equity drawdown. The reasoning here is that if the fund manager maintains a strict, disciplined adherence to the trading system and the market subsequently fails to exceed the historical worst peak-to-valley equity drawdown, then commitment of additional investment dollars into such an environment actually represents lower risk and a greater potential for profit than could normally be achieved through implementation of the system.

But what if the largest historical drawdown from the backtested period is violated? Either this can mean that our system's integrity remains intact and we simply need to scale down our volumetric exposure to adjust for unprecedented levels of performance volatility, or it can serve as a warning that the dynamics of the market may be shifting and our system should be modified or perhaps no longer traded. Determining which of these two possibilities we are facing illustrates the importance of pairing robust mechanical trading systems with experienced traders and risk managers who are well versed at utilizing the price risk management tools discussed in this chapter.

CHAPTER 9

Improving the Rate of Return

Improving Returns by Expanding the Comfort Zone

The superior man bends his attention to what is radical. That being established, all practical courses naturally grow up.

—Confucius

THREE TYPES OF DIVERSIFICATION

Diversification is among the most important and underutilized tools available to traders and investors because it allows improvement of our rates of return without proportionately increasing risk assumed to achieve these enhanced levels of performance. The most commonly employed type of diversification—asset class diversification—has already been discussed in Chapters 3 and 4, where we looked at how diversification among assets that had low correlations improved our overall performance. A review of Tables 3.2 to 3.13 and Tables 4.4 to 4.8 shows that diversification almost always yielded improvements when compared with the performance of individual assets.

This chapter focuses on the two other diversification methodologies: adaptation of different parameter sets for the same trading system and combining of negatively and/or uncorrelated trading systems.

DIVERSIFICATION OF PARAMETER SETS

Assuming that a trading account has adequate equity under management, it is preferable to diversify parameter sets rather than to trade multiple contracts with the same parameter set. Although there maybe strong positive correlations between parameter sets of the same trading system, Tables 7.1 to 7.20 show that even minor modifications to parameter sets can make the difference between an overall profitable or losing outcome. Furthermore, as shown in Chapter 7, because we can never be certain as to which parameter set will outperform in the future, parameter set diversification greatly aids in minimizing regret. Minimization of regret in this context strengthens our psychological ability to adhere to a disciplined and consistent (e.g., systematic and/or mechanical) approach toward trading.[2]

A comparison of Tables 9.1 and 9.2 exemplifies this final point. Table 9.1 shows the results of various parameter sets on the two moving average crossover system for IMM Swiss franc during the in-sample period of 1993

TABLE 9.1 Moving average crossover optimization for CME Swiss franc (1993–2002).

Short Moving Average	Long Moving Average	P:MD
10	*29*	*1.76*
9	29	1.44
8	32	1.41
9	32	1.39
10	32	1.30
10	26	1.10
8	29	1.07
8	26	0.91
9	**26**	**0.72**
9	23	0.56
6	26	0.48
7	26	0.44
7	29	0.35
10	20	0.25
8	23	−0.11
9	20	−0.15
10	23	−0.18
8	20	−0.19
7	32	−0.19
6	23	−0.24
6	29	−0.24
7	23	−0.36
6	32	−0.45
7	20	−0.73
6	*20*	*−0.83*

Note: All trade summaries include $100 round-turn trade deductions for slippage and commissions. Data source: CQG, Inc.

TABLE 9.2 Moving average crossover optimization for CME Swiss franc—out of sample study (2003).

Short Moving Average	Long Moving Average	P:MD
7	20	0.83
6	26	0.77
10	23	0.71
7	32	0.70
6	23	0.63
8	32	0.58
7	26	0.55
7	23	0.54
8	23	0.50
6	32	0.47
10	32	0.46
9	20	0.45
8	29	0.40
10	20	0.36
9	32	0.36
6	*20*	*0.28*
8	20	0.26
7	29	0.24
9	23	0.20
8	26	0.16
10	26	0.16
6	29	0.11
9	**26**	**−0.02**
9	29	−0.13
10	*29*	*−0.36*

Note: All trade summaries include $100 round-turn trade deductions for slippage and commissions. Data source: CQG, Inc.

to 2002. Notice that the best-performing parameter set in this Table was the 10- and 29-day moving average crossover; the second-to-worst-performer was the 7- and 20-day parameter set. Compare this with Table 9.2, which is the same system on the IMM Swiss franc for the out-of-sample year of 2003. Not only is the best-performing parameter set of our in-sample period now the *worst* performer, but also our second-to-worst in-sample performer has now become the top-performing parameter set.

Table 9.2 is even more instructive in the context of diversification when we compare the performance of the 7- and 20-day and the 6- and 20-day parameter sets. Although these parameter sets retained identical longer-term moving average parameters and the shorter-term moving average parameter was changed only by one step, the 7- and 20-day parameter set was the year's top performer, while the 6- and 20-day parameter set remained in the bottom half of all parameter sets analyzed.

MECHANICS OF TRADING SYSTEM DIVERSIFICATION

Diversification of negatively and/or uncorrelated trading systems is one of the most effective methods of improving rates of return without proportionately increasing the risk assumed to achieve these enhanced levels of performance. To illustrate this point, let us examine a trend-following system from Chapter 3 (MACD) with our diversified futures portfolio, and a directionally biased intermediate-term mean reversion system from Chapter 4 (RSI Extremes with the 200-day moving average filter) with our mean reversion portfolio, and then compare these results with the combined performance of both trading systems.

In comparing Tables 9.3 and 9.4 to Table 9.5, the first and most important improvement is in the profit to maximum drawdown ratio. This is due to the fact that low correlations between the trend-following and mean reversion systems led to a smoothing of equity drawdowns for the performance of the combined trading system results. Although the maximum drawdown column shown in Table 9.5 was larger than in Table 9.3 or 9.4, it represented an increase only of roughly 17 percent and 20 percent respectively. By contrast, because Table 9.5 took all signals generated by both systems, its total net profits were additive, thereby leading to an overall improvement in performance results.

TABLE 9.3   MACD totals from 1993 to 2002.

Asset	Profit	# Trades	# Days	Max Draw	MDD	MCL	P:MD	P:L Ratio	%W	Time %
Total	219498	175	142.9	−42554	686	7	5.16	2.34	42.85	100

Note: All trade summaries include $100 round-turn trade deductions for slippage and commissions. Data source: CQG, Inc.

TABLE 9.4   RSI extremes with 200-day moving average filter and 2.5% stop. Totals from 1993 to 2002.

Asset	Profit	# Trades	# Days	Max Draw	MDD	MCL	P:MD	P:L Ratio	%W	Time %
Totals	100188	372	20.4	−44202	801	11	2.27	1.27	54.57	31.06

Note: All trade summaries include $100 round-turn trade deductions for slippage and commissions. Data source: CQG, Inc.

TABLE 9.5 Combination of MACD totals and RSI extremes totals from 1993 to 2002.

Asset	Profit	# Trades	# Days	Max Draw	MDD	MCL	P:MD	P:L Ratio	%W	Time %
Totals	319686	547	59.6	−53487	1084	14	5.98	1.61	50.82	53.12

Note: All trade summaries include $100 round-turn trade deductions for slippage and commissions. Data source: CQG, Inc.

In addition, combining these uncorrelated trading programs lessened many of the deficiencies of both methodologies as stand-alone systems. For example, one of the drawbacks to the trend-following system as a stand-alone solution is that it experiences more losing trades than winners. By contrast, by combining these two systems, the winning trade percentage increased from 42.85 percent for trading the MACD system alone to 50.82 percent.

Because these two trading systems are not highly correlated, sometimes both will generate profits; sometimes one will profit while the other loses; and sometimes both will lose. Consequently, the only way to replicate the backtested performance of these combined system results is through consistent implementation of all signals generated by all assets and/or trading systems. In other words, traders should not try to outguess the systems.

Although consistent implementation of all signals for all assets sounds like a straightforward proposition, it is complicated by the fact that both systems could be trading the same asset. In fact, this was the case for the combined trading system results generated in Table 9.5, because both the trend-following and mean reversion portfolios contained the E-mini S&P 500 futures contract. Consequently it is quite possible that these two trading systems could have generated opposite trading signals for the same instrument.

When I first started trading multiple systems with low correlations, I encountered this problem of conflicting trading signals. I failed to take a buy signal in the trend-following system because my mean reversion system had generated a sell signal for the same instrument. During the overnight trading session, my mean reversion realized its profit, which corresponded to what would have been a temporary open equity drawdown in the trend-following system (had I taken that trade). Then, almost immediately after the mean reversion system's profitable exit, the market reversed, and I awoke to find that I had missed out on one of that year's most profitable trend trades.

This painful lesson reinforced the fact that a prerequisite to successful implementation of diversified trading strategies is never missing a trading signal. Subsequently I have found that the simplest and preferred solution to this problem of conflicting signals for the same asset is the maintenance of two (or more) separate trading accounts—one for each distinct trading methodology (e.g., trend-following, intermediate-term mean reversion, short-term).

PSYCHOLOGY OF TRADING SYSTEM DIVERSIFICATION

Years of empirical observation have led me to firmly believe that there are at least three distinct trading personalities: trend-following, mean reversion, and short-term (e.g., swing trading, day trading) trading. Yet nothing prevents us from expanding beyond our natural center of gravity (see Chapter 6 to determine the innate trading personality) and adopting the trading strategies of the other basic personality types. Although I feel adoption of intermediate-term mean reversion trading systems is easier for either the trend-trading or short-term trading personalities, I believe that, with practice, a person can adapt and master any of these personalities (although each person's natural center of gravity probably will continue to feel the most comfortable).

I believe that traders should incorporate a different trading style only after they achieve long-standing success with their natural center of gravity. We must master the type of trading system that addresses our psychological strengths (e.g., quick mindedness, patience, contrarianism, etc.) to build confidence and strengthen discipline. We nurture the good trading habits necessary for success in the easiest environment possible, and then, and only then, do we apply the universal rules of discipline and money management to the type of trading that seems foreign.

Although at first glance it seems simple enough merely to add another style of trading to our arsenal, with the exception of the transition from undisciplined gambling to consistently disciplined, rule-based speculation, this idea of combining noncorrelated trading systems is the greatest challenge most traders will ever face.

Imagine that you are a successful trend trader who has made a good living in the markets for several years. You have had several years of positive reinforcement for buying recent highs and/or selling lows, for taking numerous small losses and letting profits run. Now you attempt to add intermediate-term mean reversion trading to your core trend-following strategy.

Typically here is what happens: Your trend trading strategy has you selling the euro against the U.S. dollar, and you do so with the utmost confidence. The trend unfolds nicely and profits start to accumulate. Then the mean reversion system signals a buy of the euro currency against the Japanese yen. For the last three years you have never deviated from a signal generated by your system(s), but suddenly you hesitate. You are already making money with your trend-following system by selling euros, so even though you have tested the mean reversion system and intellectually know that the combination of negatively and/or uncorrelated systems improves overall performance, you decide not to take the mean reversion system's signal.

This single inaction in the face of a trading signal subverts years of disciplined trading. Suddenly all of the old psychological problems that haunted your early career as a trader reemerge because you are fighting the basic premises that have led to your recent success.

If that story sounds familiar, do not despair. It may take a few missed signals and much review of backtested results before you gain the confidence and discipline necessary to simultaneously take trend-following, mean reversion, and/or short-term signals of highly correlated assets. At the outset, participating in and fading a trend simultaneously is a highly unnatural and uncomfortable endeavor. In fact, many traders find the practice so foreign and stressful that they simply abandon system diversification and revert to what is comfortable and has worked for them in the past.

Although there is absolutely nothing wrong with adhering to a single successful trading methodology, personal growth and heightened success in trading comes from psychological flexibility and ability to behave consistently in an uncomfortable and unnatural manner. One of the best tools to help us in modifying our behavior is a thorough review of the backtested results from system diversification, including risk/reward quantification and other comparative analyses similar to those shown in Tables 9.3 to 9.5.

In addition, it is also helpful to remember that our initial success as a trader stemmed from our ability to do the unnatural, uncomfortable thing. Incorporation of trading systems that are antithetical to our innate trading personality is merely the natural extension of the same skill set that led to our initial success as traders.

Finally, by expanding their trading vocabulary to include systems that specifically target weaknesses in their psychological makeup, short-term traders learn patience, while longer-term traders master quick-mindedness. The ability to transcend our innate center of gravity by adopting trading systems that are antithetical to our personalities challenges not only habit-based behaviors but also core belief systems. Such challenges can have profound and lasting consequences to our lives both within and beyond the markets.

CHAPTER 10

Discretion and Systems Trading

Discretion within a Mechanical Framework

Contradiction is not a sign of falsity, nor the lack of contradiction a sign of truth.

—Pascal

The issue of discretion within the context of a mechanical trading system is always a controversial matter, because its inclusion could lead to a breakdown in trader discipline and consistency. During the developmental stages of this manuscript, I debated omitting the topic of trader discretion to prevent a discounting of my emphasis on consistency and discipline in trading. It is to prevent readers from discounting the importance of consistency and discipline in trading that I introduce the subject only after laying the groundwork in terms of the preeminent importance of maintaining a disciplined approach to execution of trading signals.

The market's propensity to experience paradigms shifts and price shock events largely led me to decide to retain this chapter. Excluding the issue of trader discretion within the context of a mechanical trading system could lead readers to be unprepared and/or complacent. Although it may be true that adherence to the principles of sound money management (as outlined in Chapter 8) can allow systematic traders to avoid ruin during paradigm shifts and/or price shocks, this ability to "survive" is probably a suboptimal solution to the employment of mechanical trading systems.

DISCRETION AND PARADIGM SHIFTS

Although there is no objective answer to the question of what constitutes a paradigm shift in market dynamics, for the purposes of this book I will

185

define the phenomenon as a permanent or long-term shift in market behavior that greatly diminishes the viability of historically robust trading models. In Chapter 7, I presented an example of a paradigm shift through the comparison of Figures 7.1 and 7.2, which illustrated a collapse in the performance of the 20-day channel breakout system for IGBPUSD (British pound–U.S. dollar) from 1993 to 2002 versus 1983 to 2002.

When faced with paradigm shifts, mechanically generated trading signals could (depending on the size of system stop-loss levels employed) result in the termination of a system trader's career. Recognition of the potential severity of this problem has led to the establishment of some possible thresholds for the introduction of a discretionary overlay to the implementation of mechanical trading systems.

Some of these potential thresholds are, in fact, objectively quantifiable (and therefore mechanical) and were alluded to in Chapter 8. They include exceeding the maximum number of consecutive losses experienced by the system during its backtested history and exceeding of the system's worst peak-to-valley equity drawdown and stop-loss levels for trading systems. In such instances, a prudent discretionary course of action probably would entail suspending execution of signals generated by the trading system, or, at the very least, reducing volumetric exposure to the floundering system (until the market dynamics in question reasserted themselves).

DISCRETION, VOLATILITY, AND PRICE SHOCKS

Just as there are no objective criteria for what constitutes a paradigm shift, neither are there any for price shock events. Instead, I have found it useful to develop a hybrid discretionary-objective overlay for my mechanical trading systems that is based on highly aberrant increases in volatility. Whether the rest of the investment community decides that a particular increase in volatility was a price shock or not is irrelevant to me. Instead, the key is employing a robust criterion that forces me to reduce my exposure to market environments that could endanger my trading career.

Although there are certainly arbitrary numerical thresholds—such as a 50 percent increase in one-year historical volatility levels—that could trigger a reduction of volumetric exposure, because volatility exhibits both trending and cyclical tendencies, I hesitate to limit my definition of an aberrant increase in volatility to any static numerical threshold. Instead, I argue that a more robust solution to the issue of determining volatility thresholds includes the overlaying of a discretionary filter onto the objective, percentage-based threshold of a 50 percent increase in one-year historical volatility levels.

For example, if a 45 percent increase in one-year historical volatility is the direct result of an ultra-short-term, unsustainable headline-driven event (e.g., the capture of Saddam Hussein), then scaling back of volumetric exposure is probably unwarranted. By contrast, if a 20 percent increase in one-year historical volatility is the result of something that the trader determines to be due to an intermediate- or long-term shift in market dynamics (e.g., legislation leading to a shift in supply and demand), then a volumetric scaling back of exposure might prove a preferable course of action as opposed to waiting for the static 50 percent increase in volatility threshold to be breached.

In either instance, the introduction of discretion into the mechanical trading framework did not represent an abandonment of a disciplined response to the signals generated by the trading systems. Furthermore, unless the increase in volatility is so severe that the prudent course of action (based on equity under management) precludes continued participation in that particular market, the introduction of a discretionary filter merely results in a potential reduction in volumetric exposure to the trading signals generated by the system(s).

Of course, the introduction of the 50 percent increase in historical volatility threshold is merely one of innumerable objective criteria that could be used as a trigger for reducing volumetric exposures. In fact, Chapters 7 and 8 alluded to other potentially useful thresholds, including environments in which historical profit levels are exceeded by over 150 percent, along with the breakdown of historically stable correlations.

MECHANICAL DISCRETION

If the introduction of trader discretion ultimately could result in the abandonment of a successful mechanical system and if blind adherence to a mechanical approach could yield suboptimal results if a price shock or paradigm shift occurs, perhaps the answer is to create a comprehensive set of rules that would dictate when trader discretion could be introduced. Although such rules are virtually infinite, some ideal candidates include increases in volatility beyond a specified percentage threshold, exceeding the maximum number of consecutive losses in the system's backtested history, and achievement of unprecedented per-trade profit levels.

All examples of objective criteria for the introduction of discretionary elements provide a more robust price risk management methodology. As long as we allow stringent adherence to the principles of price risk management to remain our blotter test, the introduction of a discretionary element into our arsenal of trading techniques cannot degenerate into many of the common flaws of novice discretionary trading (e.g., inability to cut losses, increasing position size after losses, etc.).

PROS AND CONS OF "TRUE" DISCRETION

So far I have addressed only the issue of objectively quantifiable criteria to introduce discretionary overrides for mechanical trading systems as defined by the trading system's backtested results and/or the historical volatility of the assets traded. Once I include quantifiable fundamentals, such as purchasing power parity,[1] sentiment indicators (e.g., put-call ratios, commitment of traders reports, etc.),[2] and interest rate differentials, or "fuzzy" fundamentals, such as headline news events, the value of including such discretionary overrides becomes somewhat murkier.

This does not mean that the utilization of fuzzier discretionary overrides on a mechanical trading system is without merit. Instead, I am simply pointing out that inclusion of such overrides could call into question the continued validity our trading system's in- and out-of-sample results. Furthermore, once such results are no longer indisputable, risk tolerance measures such as maximum consecutive losses and profit to maximum drawdown ratios also become problematic.

There are and, in all likelihood, there will continue to be obvious moments in which traditional discretionary overrides are prudent performance enhancement tools. While I recognize and freely acknowledge this fact, I merely add a note of caution that once discipline has been overridden without violation of some objectively quantifiable threshold, a dangerous psychological precedent is set in motion. As a result, until traders successfully demonstrate their ability to sustain consistent, disciplined adherence to a mechanical trading system over a prolonged period of time, I suggest that they reject fuzzier discretionary overrides in favor of simple, objectively quantifiable rules of entry and exit.

CHAPTER 11

Psychology of Mechanical Trading

Trading Systems and Transformational Psychology

I count him braver who overcomes his desires than him who conquers his enemies; for the hardest victory is over self.

—Aristotle

DISCIPLINE AND FLEXIBILITY

Although discipline and flexibility might sound like mutually exclusive terms, as I have shown in Chapter 10, this is not the case. Traders must be disciplined enough to consistently execute trades irrespective of personal winning or losing streaks, bullish or bearish market consensus. Such a disciplined approach usually entails mastery of open-mindedness so that they can continuously view things differently from the crowd. Moreover, mechanical traders must be flexible enough to abandon their disciplined adherence to a trading system once that system is no longer robust enough to generate profits (due to a paradigm shift in market behavior).

Zen Buddhist philosophers often attempt to explain the nonlinear nature of reality with paradoxical phrases: true, false, both and neither, all at the same time. Although at first glance the phrases seem nonsensical, it is the essence of the multidimensional nature of all things, including market behavior. Moreover, the phrase epitomizes the flexible mind-set of successful traders. For example, I can state: "It is true that traders succeed by following the trend." Yes, this is true for trend traders, but it is false for nondirectionally biased mean reversion traders. Next, I can say that the statement is both true and false because some system traders employ both trend-following and nondirectionally biased mean reversion models simultaneously. Then it could be argued that for other market participants, such as market makers, the statement is neither true nor false, because their ability to capture the spread between the bid and offer, as opposed to either the trending or mean reverting nature of the markets, leads to their success. Finally, when examining the entire spectrum of market participants, all of these statements are true at the same time.

This is the nature of the markets, expressing the many faces of their ever-changing higher truth. It is a higher truth in that it transcends dualistic notions of yes, no or true, false. This is why success in the markets has so many manifestations: trending, mean reverting, long term, intermediate term, swing trading, day trading, scalping, and so on. It is also why the market sometimes rewards and sometimes punishes the same behavior.

For those thinking that this section confirms the argument of random walk theorists, let me say in the true Zen Buddhist tradition that it simultaneously does and does not. Although it is true that there are some moments of randomness within the ever-changing face of the market, such short-term randomness in no way invalidates the market's eternally repetitive patterns of trending and mean reverting market behavior.

It is because we can never know with certainty whether the market is in its mean reverting or trending phase, nor when it is changing from one to the other, that flexibility and open-mindedness are so crucial to success as a trader. The more we can allow for any possible outcome in the markets, the easier it will be for us to quickly admit when we are wrong and thereby accept small losses, let large winners run, and adapt to whatever the market is currently showing as its reality and truth.

The market has the potential to accelerate psychological and spiritual growth because it forces us to relinquish illusions and embrace the ever-changing nature of reality. A close friend and longtime colleague, Richard Hom, goes so far as to call participation in the markets *reality therapy*. In many arenas of life, illusions can be nurtured and coddled indefinitely. In the markets, however, illusions of being right are punished mercilessly and relentlessly until abandoned in favor of reality.[1] Many careers never force us to admit our failures or accept responsibility for errors. Although pursuit of such livelihoods may sound satisfying to the fragile ego, they are intellectual, emotional, and spiritual dead ends. We grow through our failures and admission of fallibility; we mature by embracing humility and being nonattached to the results of our actions; we succeed by shattering illusions of control and flowing with the ever-changing nature of reality.

Can a person succeed as a trader without adopting this seemingly chaotic and unsettling view of the market? Of course. Because of the market's multidimensional nature, with discipline, determination, and patience people can adapt to one level of its truth and enjoy a certain degree of success. In this way the market is similar to the doctrines of higher truth found throughout the great religious traditions.

Such religious literature is filled with phrases offering different levels of truth to various people. For example, "judge not, lest ye be judged" reveals a lesson regarding ethical law that is grasped—though, like success in the markets, not easily practiced—by the entire congregation. Yet spiritual adepts simultaneously perceive this statement both as the commonly acknowledged moral percept and a spiritual admonition against acceptance of external reality (along with one's own nature) based on illusory surface appearances.

Although seemingly contradictory in nature, this higher truth of market behavior is an embracing of the ever-changing order within the chaos. This concept of order within the chaos, and the fact that markets are perpetually changing, is why participants find trading so stressful and why mechanical trading systems prove to be such an invaluable tool for reprogramming us to do the unnatural and uncomfortable thing. It is our ability to embrace the risk of adversity and do what is uncomfortable that leads to rewards of profit.

Mechanical trading systems work because, through repetition, they train us to embrace the unnatural until it almost becomes second nature. When a person first learned to drive, putting the car in reverse seemed counterintuitive and unnatural because the wheel turned the car in the opposite direction from when it was going forward. Yet through a combination of instruction (which included watching and listening as more adept drivers walked the person through the process) and experience gained through repetition of the task, the unnatural eventually became natural.

FLEXIBILITY IN BODY AND MIND

Many somatic practices (martial arts, Feldenkrais, Alexander technique, etc.) believe that the body reprograms the mind and vice versa. It is interesting that the practice known in India as *hatha yoga*, which specifically addresses the idea of spiritual union through exertion of physical force, is more commonly known throughout the "intellectually focused" West simply as yoga, or union. Union of the mind and body is an integral aspect of our growth and evolution. This is why Chapter 5 emphasized the importance of physical exercise as a method of alleviating stress and maintaining balance in both trading and life in general.

Obviously the strength of human beings lies in our ability to achieve anything that we focus on with single-mindedness. Nevertheless, our sense of peace and wellness are indisputably enhanced by fitness of body and mind. If your goal is the achievement of greater flexibility in mind, practice various physical activities to ensure flexibility of the body (and vice versa).

KNOWING OURSELVES

Trading offers us a tremendous opportunity to learn about ourselves. This is why I strongly encourage traders to keep a journal. It serves as an objective record of our emotions and prejudices regarding market behavior. Once we can make an accurate assessment of these biases and emotional pitfalls, we can work on changing our intellectual attitudes and emotional responses to the market.

For many, trading is an endless cycle of manias and depressions. Because the market is an ever-changing objective truth, emotions such as euphoria after gains or despair following losses merely drain us of our ability to perform effectively in the future. Instead, utilization of mechanical trading systems trains us to practice even-mindedness and nonattachment to the results of our actions. Eventually, consistent adherence to the entry and exit signals generated by our trading models frees us from the emotional roller-coaster of undisciplined trading and replaces it with feelings of satisfaction after achieving a profit and (assuming we correctly executed our system) acceptance and emotional resiliency following a loss.

One concept that I personally find useful in assisting me to remain even-minded following a loss is to remember that I am in the market for the long haul and that the result of a single trade is virtually inconsequential when compared with the next 300 trades. Instead of profit or loss on a particular trade, success as a systems trader should be measured by how well we adhere to the rules of the strategy. If we followed the rules, even though the outcome on a particular trade was a loss, we were successful. As long as the system works in the long run, and as long as traders continue to adhere to principles of solid price risk management, their survival will be ensured beyond the occurrence of a loss or even a string of losses. The laws of probability and the immutable nature of human behavior (on which virtually all successful trading strategies are based) suggest a high probability of the account's return to profitability.

If, on the other hand, we did not follow the rules, we must recognize our failure and look at what would have been the outcome had we remained disciplined. Then we must forgive ourselves, let go, and resolve to be more disciplined at the occurrence of the system's next trading signal.

In both cases—whether we adhered to our system and suffered a loss or if we failed to follow the rules—the key was an honest assessment of our actions in the market and an embracing of our emotional response to the loss or our failure. Then, after we honor the emotion, we can release the experience either by acknowledging that successful system traders suffer losses or by telling ourselves that it is okay to fail (while simultaneously resolving to implement the system on its next signal).

Many traders hope that adoption of mechanical trading systems will somehow eliminate emotions. Even-mindedness is not the elimination of emotions; it is the *tempering* of emotionalism. We are not automatons, nor should we strive to become so. Emotions are an integral aspect of our humanity. We need to honor and accept our emotional responses to events by embracing the emotions as we feel them. Then, once we have accepted, embraced, and integrated the emotion, we can practice nonattachment to the result of our actions by releasing the emotion.

This concept of embracing and releasing is in stark contrast to our usual responses of wallowing in the emotion until it eventually results in the disempowerment of our future effectiveness or denying our emotions and having them fester and subvert the confidence and single-minded pursuit of success within our conscious and subconscious minds.

SINGLE-MINDEDNESS: UNRAVELING THE ONION LAYERS

My grandfather used to tell a story about the cow that would kick over its pail after each milking. Such stories reveal much about human nature and trader psychology. Successful trading has as its prerequisite that traders are single-minded in their pursuit of success. The only obstacle to success in trading is the trader. Like my grandfather's cow, conflicted traders often are able to enjoy profits and even achieve a limited level of success, but because of various unresolved psychological conflicts, they either surrender these profits or create an artificial ceiling to their successes.

The reasons for these internal conflicts can be as varied as life itself. One trader I know kept sabotaging his successes because he was in a bad marriage and felt his success would have enriched an undeserving spouse. In such instances, it is almost impossible to trade effectively. We must believe that everyone benefiting from our success (including us) deserves it or we will continue to kick over the pail of milk. Single-mindedness sounds like an easy accomplishment; instead, it is a continuous process of self-assessment and refinement.

Although the obstacles to single-mindedness are virtually infinite, I also believe every single internal psychological block to our success stems from a single issue: self-worth. Whether we deny ourselves success because we erroneously think money is evil[2] or because our success would result in the enrichment of undeserving others, these are all reflections of the more basic internal conflict: We do not believe ourselves worthy. Although outwardly it was true that my trader friend sabotaged himself so that his spouse would suffer, why did he marry someone who was incapable of loving him in the first place? Because he did not feel he deserved a loving relationship. Why do some people believe money is evil? Because they do not think they deserve it. What prevents our recognition and embracing of the divinity within? Lack of self-worth.

Because these blocks to single-mindedness are usually unconscious, how do we know whether we as traders are conflicted in terms of our desire to succeed? We can objectively determine the answer by examining how well we adhere to rules of entry, exit, and money management. Any deviation from these rules means we need to examine why we feel unworthy of success, Then we must embrace and honor these feelings and finally release them as old programming that is inconsistent with our new self-image.

How do we transform our self-image and begin to feel worthy of success? Although this is an ever-changing process, the first and most important step is to surround ourselves with like-minded people. If a tuning fork that is oscillating at a particular frequency is placed next to one that is still, soon they both oscillate at the same frequency. If we surround ourselves with loving and supportive people, we become more loving, both of ourselves and of others.

INTUITION VERSUS THE PSYCHIC TRADER SYNDROME

Many well-respected books on trading techniques advocate the use of intuition as an adjunct to various techniques, such as fundamental and/or technical analysis. Chapter 3 specifically identified one of the potential psychological pitfalls of trend trading as an unwillingness to relinquish a portion of unrealized gains and stated that this weakness was linked with an unrealistic belief in our psychic ability to predict future market behavior. Obviously these two concepts—intuition and the psychic trader syndrome—are contradictory in nature. This is why I have purposely avoided the issue of intuition in trading decisions until I had laid the foundation of the multidimensional nature of markets and trader psychology.

Now I can provide readers with a complete exposition of my beliefs in this regard. Yes, I do feel that intuition has a place in the world of successful trading and freely acknowledge that certain traders successfully utilize this tool to enhance trading performance. Unfortunately, I also feel that a much larger number of traders use this belief in the power of intuition as an excuse to abandon their discipline in the markets.

I cannot resolve this conflict between true intuition and the delusional psychological pitfall that I describe as the psychic trader syndrome. Instead, I simply acknowledge the virtually infinite manifestations of successful trading in the markets and admit that in order for me personally to succeed as a trader, I must practice disciplined adherence to my systems, which are based on the laws of probability. Yes, I admit that certain traders are able to distinguish between intuition and imagination consistently, but, unfortunately, I do not consistently count myself among them.

If we have unyielding confidence in our ability to consistently distinguish between intuition and imagination, and if this confidence can be substantiated through documented records of successful past market forecasts, then and only then should we consider abandoning disciplined adherence to strategies and the laws of probability. The good news is that until that day arrives, as long as we can religiously adhere to sound principles of price risk management, we have a better than average probability of enjoying considerable success with a wide variety of strategies.

TRANSFORMATION VIA ADHERENCE TO MECHANICAL TRADING SYSTEMS

The personality traits that sabotage trader success are manifold but generally can be categorized in this way:

- *Lack of discipline and/or inconsistency.* The key to transformation of this trait is elimination of blocks to single-mindedness, and review of how (in general) the markets reward us for following and punish us for deviating from the rules of entry, exit, and money management.
- *Euphoria and/or greed.* Here our discipline breaks down as profits accumulate. We break the rules of exit or of money management due to impatience and a lack of respect for the market's ability to turn profits into losses. Transformation of this personality flaw is linked with our ability to practice even-mindedness. If we can reprogram ourselves to act the same way when the market generates profits as when it produces losses, then we will not abandon discipline during a large win or winning streak.
- *Fear, inability to initiate, and/or the perfect trader syndrome.* The flip side to greed and euphoria are fear and an inability to take trading signals. This can occur due to an unwillingness to fade the crowd, fear of losses, or fear of relinquishing profits. Here the key to transformation is nonattachment, to act without attachment to the results of our actions. We must forget about whether the trade will result in a profit or loss, because the result of that action only exists in an unknowable future. Instead we must focus on the present moment; now in this present moment we have received an entry signal based on either a high probability of a superior profit/loss ratio (trend trading) or an

attractive winning percentage ratio (mean reversion system). We must embrace the fear and then release it through nonattachment to the results of our actions.

TRANSFORMATIONAL PROCESS: IN LIFE AND THE MARKETS

Throughout this book, I have put forth the theory of resonance. Although a book about success in the markets is, in and of itself, a worthwhile endeavor, my reason for writing this book was intimately linked with this concept of resonance between the markets and the human experience in general.

It is my firm belief that what holds true in microcosmic spheres such as the trading realm often resonate with higher truths regarding the macrocosmic aspects of life in general. This belief forced me to continue trading despite early experiences of failure and self-doubt. I was certain that such losses and professional turmoil in my trading career somehow resonated with a greater spiritual disharmony that required resolution. Of course I could have simply stopped trading, but I had always felt that "what we resist, persists." Therefore, issues raised by trading such as lack of discipline, inconsistency, fear, and greed would resurface in one form or another until I had mastered them.

So I continued to strive toward self-mastery and success in the trading realm despite losses and frustration. Finally, after years of struggling, eventually I was able to employ a consistent, disciplined approach to trading. As I had expected, the mastery of my emotions in this particular endeavor lead to greater harmony in all other aspects of my life.

When I first mastered the discipline and consistency required for success as a trader, I erroneously assumed that trading would become easy. Instead I discovered that although I now had the experience and discipline to stay with my systems irrespective of a particular trade's outcome, my emotional response toward the practice of sticking with any particular trade periodically shifted from effortless adherence to an almost unbearable temptation to abandon my discipline. Although the severity of these emotional shifts has diminished over time, to this day they remain an integral aspect of my experience as a trader.

Such emotional shifts from temptation to abandon discipline to near-effortless adherence reminded me of a particular aspect of market behavior: retracements within the trend (see Chapter 1). Just as the market shifts from near-parabolic moves in the direction of the long-term trend, then pulls back as that trend temporarily overextends itself, I believe that our consciousness evolves through similar cycles of growth and contraction.

Some philosophical and religious traditions compare this process to a circle (or wheel) in which growth is followed by contraction ad infinitum.

Instead, I contend that the evolutionary process only "feels" like a circle as we perpetually shift from one end of the spectrum to its opposite. In fact, the process is more like a spiral, in which we revisit variations of these same struggles over and again, yet each successive test of our consciousness with these same behavioral archetypes is in fact occurring at ever higher octaves of consciousness until the experiences eventually culminate in a paradigm shift beyond these polar opposites of the human experience that Eastern religions call enlightenment.

What is the catalyst leading to this paradigm shift? Conscious effort. This book has been dedicated to explaining various practices and techniques, all intended to strengthen our resolve to act with single-minded consciousness in pursuit of success in trading. Furthermore, I believe that this process of strengthening our will through the consistent employment of mindfulness and conscious effort in this one area of life affects all other realms of our consciousness.

How does this catalyst of conscious effort actualize the paradigm shift from dualism to even-mindedness and nonattachment to the results of our actions? When employed with discipline and consistency, conscious effort eventually leads to the maturation and ascendancy of what Eastern religions call witness consciousness. Witness consciousness is that part of us which can objectively "witness" our conscious mind's shift from dualistic poles of success and failure, mania and depression, without attraction or repulsion to either extreme. Witness consciousness is that part of us that, through mindfulness and conscious effort, enables us to transcend dualism in favor of single-mindedness and nonattachment.

In conclusion, it is my sincere hope that this book has aided readers in their quest to consistently employ conscious effort, which ultimately will lead to the strengthening of witness consciousness. Further, it is my hope that this ascendancy of witness consciousness ultimately culminates in the transcendence of whatever was preventing readers' attainment of their desired level of success in the markets and, perhaps more important, in their lives in general.

> *May beings be free from all states of no leisure*
> *And be endowed with faith, wisdom and kindness;*
> *With food (obtained in a proper manner) and excellent conduct,*
> *May they be mindful throughout their lives.*
>
> —Shantideva

Notes

Chapter 1

1. Joachim Goldberg and Rüdiger von Nitzsch, *Behavioral Finance* (Chichester, UK: John Wiley & Sons, 2001), p. 157.
2. Daniel Kahneman was awarded the Nobel Prize in economics in 2002 for his work on behavioral finance.
3. Mandelbrot first suggested that capital markets displayed a stable Paretian distribution in 1964.
4. See "Types of Technical Indicators: Trend-Following and Mean Reversion" in this chapter for a detailed explanations of Wilder's RSI and moving averages.
5. Ari Kiev, *Trading in the Zone* (New York: John Wiley & Sons, 2001), p. 162.
6. Goldberg and von Nitzsch, *Behavioral Finance*, chapter 4.
7. This section is adapted from Richard Weissman, "The Math behind the System," *Working Money*™, December 2003, ©2003 Technical Analysis, Inc. Used with permission.
8. For detailed explanations of each of these classical technical indicators, see John J. Murphy, *Technical Analysis of the Financial Markets* (Paramus, NJ: New York Institute of Finance, 1999).
9. Fundamentals are defined as supply and demand statistics and/or news events.
10. Peak-to-valley drawdowns are a more accurate measure of risk than closed-out position losses. Instead of merely quantifying declines in account equity based on closed-out profits and losses, peak-to-valley drawdowns measure deterioration from an old equity peak (or high water mark) to the ultimate trough on the basis of daily mark-to-market calculations.
11. Perhaps the most common indicator-driven trigger is the breaking of the 200-day moving average in the equities market.
12. See Paul H. Cootner, ed., *The Random Character of Stock Market Prices* (Cambridge, MA: MIT Press, 1964).
13. Based on proprietary studies, I have found that the majority of trading instruments are range-bound roughly 70 percent of the time. Of course, certain markets, such as equity indices, display an even greater propensity toward mean

reversion, while others, such as foreign currencies, show a greater tendency toward long, sustainable trending action.

14. See Chapter 2 for a detailed explanation.

15. J. Welles Wilder, *New Concepts in Technical Trading Systems* (Greensboro, NC: Trend Research, 1978).

Chapter 2

1. This ability to trade against the crowd at temporary or long-term market extremes is the most well-publicized form of contrarianism and leads many to erroneously believe that contrarianism is synonymous with countertrend trading.

2. For explanations of linearly weighted and exponentially smoothed moving averages, see John J. Murphy, *Technical Analysis of the Financial Markets* (Paramus, NJ: New York Institute of Finance, 1999), p. 199.

3. Perry J. Kaufman, *Smarter Trading* ((New York: McGraw-Hill, 1995), pp. 129–153.

4. Other variations of whipsaw waiting periods include time delays. Time delays require the market to close beyond the signal price after a specified number of days.

5. See Jack D. Schwager, *Schwager on Futures: Technical Analysis* (New York: John Wiley & Sons, 1996), chapter 20.

6. Chapter 3 analyzes the limitations of tools such as ADX and volatility measures.

7. Chapter 4 covers various exit strategies for mean reversion trading systems in detail.

8. See Schwager, *Schwager on Futures: Technical Analysis*, p. 619.

9. For a more comprehensive explanation of DMI, see J. Welles Wilder, *New Concepts in Technical Trading Systems* (Greensboro, NC: Trend Research, 1978).

10. For a more detailed explanation, see Murphy, *Technical Analysis of the Financial Markets*, pp. 381–384.

11. Ibid., pp. 215–216.

12. Perry J. Kaufman, *Trading Systems and Methods*, 3rd ed. (New York: John Wiley & Sons, 1998).

Chapter 3

1. See Jack D. Schwager, *Schwager on Futures: Technical Analysis* (New York: John Wiley & Sons, 1996), chapter 12, for a more detailed explanation.

2. Thomas Stridsman, *Trading Systems That Work* (New York: McGraw-Hill, 2001), pp. 37–38.

3. For example, the CME changed the point value of the S&P 500 contract from 500 to 250 times the index price following close of business on October 31, 1997, in response to the increase in valuation and volatility of the instrument.

4. Frank J. Fabozzi and Irving M. Pollack, eds., *The Handbook of Fixed Income Securities*, 6th ed. (New York: McGraw-Hill, 2000).

5. My studies thus far have been limited to linear instruments, but the application of an implied volatility filter to simple trend-following systems such as those showcased in this chapter seems like a worthwhile experiment.

6. Art Collins, "Making Money with Momentum," *Futures* (August 2003): 45.

7. See Chapter 4 for stop-loss programming code. Also, whenever channel breakout is changed from the original stop and reverse system through the addition of other exit criteria, readers may want to consider unchecking the "allow entry on exit" box. Because the programming software cannot determine whether stops or entry orders were filled first on daily charts, unchecking this box lessens the severity of erroneous results in the backtested data.

8. Barbara Rockefeller, *The Global Trader* (New York: John Wiley & Sons, 2001), chapter 5.

Chapter 4

1. For more details, see Thomas Stridsman, *Trading Systems That Work* (New York: McGraw-Hill, 2001), pp. 70–77 and 157–159.

Chapter 6

1. The odds are also worse than 50 percent due to the fact that both buyers and sellers lose commissions and/or slippage.

Chapter 7

1. Robert Pardo, *Design, Testing and Optimization of Trading Systems* (New York: John Wiley & Sons, 1992), p. 55.

2. Ibid., pp. 86–89.

3. Ibid., pp. 88–89.

4. Jack D. Schwager, *Schwager on Futures: Technical Analysis* (New York: John Wiley & Sons, 1996), p. 674.

5. Pardo, *Design, Testing and Optimization*, p. 3.

6. Ibid., p. 4.

7. Schwager, *Schwager on Futures*, pp. 682–694.

8. Pardo, *Design, Testing and Optimization*, p. 134.

9. Ibid., p. 141.

10. Ibid., pp. 104–106.

11. Schwager, *Schwager on Futures*, pp. 688–691.

12. Pardo, *Design, Testing and Optimization*, pp. 143–144.

13. Schwager, *Schwager on Futures*, pp. 626–629.

14. Pardo, *Design, Testing and Optimization*, pp. 78–79, 142.

15. Utilization of the most-up-to-date data for out-of-sample testing is merely the simplest solution to the walk-forward testing process. Other robust methodologies include random multiperiod data samplings.

16. Pardo, *Design, Testing and Optimization*, pp. 110–114.

17. Ibid., pp. 114–118.

18. Ibid., pp. 27–28.

19. Ibid., pp. 156–157.

20. Subtraction of the risk-free rate assumes the inability of traders to capture this rate of return while participating in the markets; this is not the case with exchange-traded futures.

21. For a more comprehensive examination of the topic, see Schwager, *Schwager on Futures*, chapter 21.

Chapter 8

1. Van K. Tharp, *Trade Your Way to Financial Freedom* (New York: McGraw-Hill, 1999).

2. Although it is sometimes argued that profits accumulated prior to the drawdown could act as a cushion to prevent the triggering of a system stop loss, this is not prudent price risk management. Instead, fund managers always must assume the infusion of investment capital subsequent to their fund's attainment of a peak (or high water mark) in account equity. Based on this assumption, such an investor would not have the luxury of any previously accrued profits to cushion the drawdown in account equity.

3. Why 12 consecutive losses instead of 10? This is because as account equity decreases, the 4 percent being risked on each position becomes a smaller dollar amount. For example, on the second trade, we would be risking .04 times the remaining $96,000, or $3,840.

4. Thomas Stridsman, *Trading Systems That Work* (New York: McGraw-Hill, 2001), pp. 272–273.

5. For a comprehensive exposition of various methods of calculating value at risk, see Kevin Robert Dowd, *Beyond Value at Risk* (Chichester, UK: John Wiley & Sons, 1998), chapters 3–5.

6. Ibid., p. 12.

7. For a more comprehensive examination of stress testing, see ibid., chapter 6.

Chapter 9

1. Portions of this chapter were adapted from Richard Weissman. "Boosting Rates of Return with Non-Correlated Systems," *Technical Analysis of STOCKS &*

COMMODITIES™, Vol. 22, No. 1 (January 2004). ©2004 Technical Analysis, Inc. Used with permission.

2. Joachim Goldberg and Rüdiger von Nitzsch, *Behavioral Finance* (Chichester, UK: John Wiley & Sons, 2001), pp. 102–106.

Chapter 10

1. See Neil Record, *Currency Overlay* (Chichester, UK: John Wiley & Sons, 2003), p. 216.

2. For a detailed explanation of these tools, see Alexander Elder, *Trading for a Living* (New York: John Wiley & Sons, 1993), chapter 7.

Chapter 11

1. R. E. McMaster, *The Art of the Trade* (New York: McGraw-Hill, 1999), p. 118.

2. As opposed to the irrational belief that money is evil, McMaster defines money as "the stored evidence of the human spirit, energy, and accumulated life over time." See ibid., p. 2.

References and Further Reading

Collins, Art. "Making Money with Momentum." *Futures* (August 2003).

Cootner, Paul H., ed. *The Random Character of Stock Market Prices.* Cambridge, MA: MIT Press, 1964.

Crouhy, Michel, Dan Galai, and Robert Mark. *Risk Management.* New York: McGraw-Hill, 2001.

Dowd, Kevin. *Beyond Value at Risk.* Chichester, UK: John Wiley & Sons, 1998.

Elder, Alexander. *Trading for a Living.* New York: John Wiley & Sons, 1993.

Evans-Wentz, W.Y. *Tibet's Great Yogi Milarepa.* London: Oxford University Press, 1928.

Fabozzi, Frank J., and Irving M. Pollack, eds. *The Handbook of Fixed Income Securities,* 6th ed. New York: McGraw-Hill, 2000.

Fusaro, Peter C., ed. *Energy Risk Management.* New York: McGraw-Hill, 1998.

Gitlin, Andrew W., ed. *Strategic Currency Investing.* Chicago: Probus, 1993.

Goldberg, Joachim, and Rüdiger von Nitzsch. *Behavioral Finance.* Chichester, UK: John Wiley & Sons, 2001.

Grinold, Richard C., and Ronald N. Kahn. *Active Portfolio Management.* 2nd ed. New York: McGraw-Hill, 2000.

Kaufman, Perry J. *Smarter Trading.* New York: McGraw-Hill, 1995.

———. *Trading Systems and Methods,* 3rd ed. New York: John Wiley & Sons, 1998.

Kiev, Ari. *Trading in the Zone.* New York: John Wiley & Sons, 2001.

LeFèvre, Edwin. *Reminiscences of a Stock Operator.* New York: John Wiley & Sons, 1994.

McMaster, R.E. *The Art of the Trade.* New York: McGraw-Hill, 1999.

Murphy, John J. *Technical Analysis of the Financial Markets.* Paramus, NJ: New York Institute of Finance, 1999.

Ouspensky, P.D. *In Search of the Miraculous.* New York: Harvest Books, 2001.

Pardo, Robert. *Design, Testing and Optimization of Trading Systems.* New York: John Wiley & Sons, 1992.

Record, Neil. *Currency Overlay.* Chichester, UK: John Wiley & Sons, 2003.

Rinpoche, Sogyal. *The Tibetan Book of Living and Dying*. San Francisco: Harper, 1992.

Rockefeller, Barbara. *The Global Trader*. New York: John Wiley & Sons, 2001.

Ruggiero, Murray A., Jr. *Cybernetic Trading Strategies*. New York: John Wiley & Sons, 1997.

Schwager, Jack D. *Market Wizards*. New York: New York Institute of Finance, 1989.

———. *The New Market Wizards*. New York: Harper Collins, 1992.

———. *Schwager on Futures: Technical Analysis*. New York: John Wiley & Sons, 1996.

Shantideva. *A Guide to the Bodhisattva's Way of Life*. New Delhi: Library of Tibetan Works and Archives, 1993.

Smithson, Charles M. *Managing Financial Risk*, 3rd ed. New York: McGraw-Hill, 1998.

Steenbarger, Brett N. *The Psychology of Trading*. Hoboken, NJ: John Wiley & Sons, 2003.

Stridsman, Thomas. *Trading Systems That Work*. New York: McGraw-Hill, 2001.

Sun Tzu. *The Art of War*. Oxford, UK: Oxford University Press, 1963.

Tharp, Van K. *Trade Your Way to Financial Freedom*. New York: McGraw-Hill, 1999.

Weissman, Richard L. "Quantifying Technical Analysis." *Energy and Power Risk Management* (May 2002).

———. "Developing Successful Mechanical Trading Systems." *Quantitative Finance* (August 2003).

———. "The Math behind the System." *Working Money* (December 2003).

———. "Boosting Rates of Return with Non-Correlated Systems." *Technical Analysis of Stocks & Commodities* (January 2004).

Wilder, J. Welles. *New Concepts in Technical Trading Systems*. Greensboro, NC: Trend Research, 1978.

Index